DECADES

Kiss

in the 1970s

Peter Gallagher

T0302674

SONICBOND

sonicbondpublishing.com

Sonicbond Publishing Limited
www.sonicbondpublishing.co.uk
Email: info@sonicbondpublishing.co.uk

First Published in the United Kingdom 2022
First Published in the United States 2022

British Library Cataloguing in Publication Data:
A Catalogue record for this book is available from the British Library

ISBN 978-1-78952-246-4

Typeset in ITC Garamond & ITC Avant Garde
Printed and bound in England

Graphic design and typesetting: Full Moon Media

DECADES

Kiss in the 1970s

Peter Gallagher

SONICBOND

sonicbondpublishing.com

Dedication

In memory of Bill McFarlane

1968 – 2022

Rock and Roll all Eternity, my friend

DECADES | Kiss in the 1970s

Contents

Introduction

The Catman. The Demon. The Spaceman. The Starchild.

In the 1970s, these four rock'n'roll superheroes were on a mission to save the nation's flaming youth from a hydra-tentacled American Scream. The strictures of a new conservative populism. Decaying inner cities. Rising crime. Tricky Dicky and Watergate. The oil crisis. The dying conflict in Vietnam and its fallout. John Denver. KISS was here to transform teenagers across all fifty states into Kings and Queens of the Night Time World, and to teach them to rock and roll all nite and party every day. At least for the playing time of two 12-inch sides of shiny black plastic, which back then could be as little as half an hour.

They weren't always known by those names, of course; they were the invention of comic books and corporate branding. The Catman might have been relatively constant, but the Spaceman was originally the Space Ace, and the Demon was the Bat Lizard. Or something. The Starchild was once The Lover, a rock and roll Rudolph Valentino with a moniker unlikely to give Doctor Doom, or anyone else, the shivers.

Before that, they were simply Peter Criss, Gene Simmons, Ace Frehley and Paul Stanley. But even these 'real' names aren't their real names, so let's start with these guys…

Peter Criss

Peter George Criscoula was born 20 December 1945. Criss grew up in a poor area of Brooklyn that was a 'melting pot of Irish and Italians and Polish and Jewish, and everyone got along fine.' Part of his pre-teen experience was typical Fiftiesville, USA – *The Lone Ranger* and *Amos 'n' Andy* on the radio, *I Love Lucy* and *Davy Crockett* on the television – and part of it less so, such as the ritual humiliation and abuse suffered at a nun-run Catholic School. The gangs came later, a violent West Side Story bereft of songs and choreography. According to his autobiography *Makeup to Breakup*, Criss graduated from the Young Lords to the Phantom Lords, had a short-lived career as a zip gunrunner, and once non-fatally stabbed a rival gang member.

Enter that rock and roll cliché, music the redeemer. When faced with the morgue slab, the jail cell, or the drum stool, who wouldn't choose the latter? Certainly not Ma Criscoula's boy Peter, nor that other kid who ran with the gang, Jerry Nolan, later of the New York Dolls and the Heartbreakers. Something that set Criscoula apart from his contemporaries, however, was his 'lightbulb moment': it wasn't Elvis Presley on *The Milton Berle Show* or The Beatles on *Ed Sullivan*, but rather hearing the Benny Goodman song 'Sing, Sing, Sing', with Gene Krupa on the drums. Krupa was Peter's idol, not Dylan or Lennon and McCartney.

Criscoula even got to open for Krupa when the band he was playing in, Joey Greco and the In Crowd, secured a summer residency at the Metropole, a once celebrated New York jazz club that was about to drop its 'just jazz' policy in the face of changing tastes. But despite his love of swing and big band, rock was what Criscoula played, and as the sixties wore on, he graduated from one dead-end band to another: The Barracudas, The Sounds of Soul, Brotherhood, Nautilus, and finally Chelsea, who briefly threatened to be something, and to whom we shall equally briefly return.

Gene Simmons

The port city of Haifa, Israel, lies 5,646 miles east of New York, as the bat-lizard flies, and it was here, on 25 August 1949, that Chaim Witz was born. His mother, Florence Klein, was one of 440,000 Hungarian Jews deported by the country's fascist Arrow Cross Party to Nazi concentration camps. Most were murdered, including Flora's mother, brother, and grandmother. After the war, she married another Jewish refugee, Ferenc Witz, and they left Europe for the newly founded state of Israel in 1948. Ferenc exits stage left a handful of years after Chaim's arrival, and in 1958 Flora and Chaim are on a plane bound for the United States, where Chaim became Eugene Klein.

Although not unsociable, young Gene's poor command of English – by his own admission, he sounded like Andy Kaufman's *Taxi* character Latka – led to a period of insularity, during which he would discover the two things that had a profound effect on shaping his later onstage persona, monster movies and comic books. He became an avid collector of DC and Marvel comics and *Famous Monsters of Filmland* magazine, and of fantasy and science fiction in general, and, with the aid of an old mimeograph, later produced his own fanzines *Fantasy News* and *Cosmos*.

Music was also part of Gene's pop culture palette, starting with Chubby Checker's 'The Twist', but really taking off with the television appearances that launched a million bands, The Beatles on *The Ed Sullivan Show* over three Sundays beginning 9 February 1964. In typical Simmons style, in his autobiography *Kiss and Make-Up*, he would claim it was the adulation of the girls in the audience rather than the Fab Four that truly grabbed his attention, but, yeah, right. Nonetheless, the 'Get Rich + Get Famous = Get Laid' formula was now rattling around in his noggin, so it was time to form a band.

Only a minuscule percentage of the groups that formed in the wake of The Beatles' US television debut made it, and Klein was in several of the millions that didn't. First, there was The Missing Links, who never made it out of high school, then the Long Island Sounds, a Top 40 covers band, notable only because it was while with them that Gene first picked up the bass. His next band, Bullfrog Bheer, the one with which he entered the 1970s, marked another stage in Klein's evolution as a musician; they too covered the hits of the day, but their setlist was now pebble-dashed with some Gene Klein originals.

Ace Frehley

Even when promoting his 2009 solo album *Anomaly*, Ace Frehley was still claiming to be from the planet Jendell, but don't believe a word of it; his birth certificate clearly states that he was born in the Bronx, New York City, right here on good ol' Terra, on 27 April 1951. And his name was Paul, not Ace.

There is a certain synchronicity to Frehley and Peter Criscoula's early teens. Both flunked school (although, bizarrely, in their respective autobiographies, they both claim to have put effort in for a short period just to demonstrate to their parents that they could get good grades, and that their academic failure was down to a lifestyle choice rather than a lack of ability. Feel free to insert another 'yeah, right' here). Both had a brief tenure in a local gang, in Frehley's case, the junior wing of the Ducky Boys, a notorious group that later served as the inspiration for the book and movie *The Wanderers*. And both were saved by music. Although he came from a musically gifted family and he was already flirting with the guitar – the first song he learned to play was the jaunty and decidedly English 'Mrs. Brown, You've Got a Lovely Daughter', a *Billboard* chart topper for Herman's Hermits in 1965 – Frehley's road to Damascus conversion occurred in the spring of 1967 at a series of daytime concerts promoted by the legendary disc jockey Murray the K. The headliners were Wilson Pickett and Mitch Ryder, but it was a couple of British outfits on the bill, The Who and Cream, that both blew Frehley away and set him on his course to become a professional musician. Then followed the usual litany of bands remembered only by those that were in them. The Four Roses. The Magic People. King Kong. Honey.

Young Frehley was a two-timer, however. Almost the moment he started his love affair with the guitar, he embarked on another long-term romance, this time with booze. It was his version of Popeye's spinach; it emboldened him through a death-defying gang initiation, it helped him overcome stage fright, and it empowered him when it came to talking to girls. In fact, he became so adept in this latter department that he began setting up his wallflower buddies with dates. 'You really help us out with the chicks, man', said one of them once (the drummer for King Kong, according to some accounts). 'You're such an ace'. And the name stuck.

Paul Stanley

By the time we get to Paul Stanley, the baby of the bunch (born Stanley Bert Eisen, 20 January 1952, Queens, New York), it all starts to sound like the same old story, same old song. Like Frehley, he 'was the wild one'. Like Simmons, he was Jewish and 'tended to be quiet and go off on my own'. Like Frehley and Criscoula, he 'was bright', but 'never got the grades' because he 'didn't feel like doing the work'. And, like Criscoula, he was a tough nut, 'a sturdy little kid' that 'nobody could really hurt'.

These quotes are all pulled from profiles of the band written by David Leaf in 1979, which eventually saw the light of day twenty-five years later in *Kiss: Behind the Mask*, an authorised biography by Leaf and Ken Sharp. Ten years after that, Stanley released his own autobiography, *Face the Music: A Life Exposed*, by which time he had matured enough to favour truth over image.

As it transpired, Stanley Eisen was someone that everyone could hurt, and many did because he was born with microtia, a congenital deformity where the external ear is underdeveloped. In Eisen's case, his right ear was little more than a stump. When he hit school age, he was ostracised because other kids couldn't accept his deformity, and victimised, the taunt of 'Stanley the one-eared monster' becoming a constant companion. Even when not suffering this verbal abuse, he could feel the eyes of others scrutinising him, and was outraged to find this was adults as often as not, whom he thought should have been more tactful and understanding. To compound matters, his right ear canal was blocked, so he was deaf in that ear also. His education suffered less because of his failure to engage with it, but because his teachers failed to compensate for his deafness, and as a result, he missed much of what was said in the classroom.

Despite this, The Beatles' legendary *Ed Sullivan* siren call also reached Stanley Eisen, and triggered the familiar need to learn an instrument, to write songs, to be in a band. It might have taken a few years, but Eisen ticked those boxes (one of his main Sixties bands deserving to make it on their name alone: Post War Baby Boom). He was also accepted into the prestigious High School of Music and Art, based on the latter rather than the former.

For anyone, being in a band and enrolled in such a Bohemian school would have been an adventure, but for Stanley Eisen, his hair grown to hide his ruined ear, these things also promised the possibility of acceptance.

1970

'Lay Down (Candles in the Rain)', Melanie Safka's paean to the Woodstock festival the previous summer, dominated the airwaves of the new decade. A month later, 'O-o-h Child' by the Five Stairsteps proved to be another smash; it was later repopularised following its inclusion in the soundtrack of *Guardians of the Galaxy* (2014) and covered by Paul Stanley's Soul Station on their 2021 debut *Now and Then*. What both these songs have in common is that they were released on the Buddah (*sic*) record label, which was managed by Neil Bogart.

By this time, twenty-seven-year-old Bogart had already enjoyed a decade of success in the music industry. In 1961, under the name Neil Scott, he scored a minor hit with a song called 'Bobby'. In 1966, he heard a song called '96 Tears' that was enjoying success in the Michigan area, bought the rights to it, and launched ? and the Mysterians to the top of the *Billboard* chart. And late in the decade, he played an important role in the rise of bubblegum music, Buddah being home to some of the genre's most successful groups, such as The Ohio Express and The 1910 Fruitgum Company.

However, a new form of music was emerging in the dwindling days of the old decade, one which dispensed with the roll and emphasised the rock. Led Zeppelin's twin releases of 1969 (*Led Zeppelin*, *Led Zeppelin II*) embraced the then-prevalent blues-rock and gave it a tougher edge, while Deep Purple jettisoned the cover versions and progressive stylings that dominated their first three albums to release *In Rock*, a defiant and unambiguous new manifesto in June 1970. Both the title and the album cover, which saw the band members replacing the four presidents on Mount Rushmore, were clear proclamations of the hard rock the band now espoused. Four months earlier, Black Sabbath released their eponymous debut, a hard rock classic regarded by many as the first heavy metal album.

Across the Atlantic, Grand Funk Railroad, pioneers of the commercially-successful-critically-derided model later perfected by Kiss, unleashed their riff-heavy brand of boogie, and The Guess Who adopted a harder rock approach on their first release of the 1970s, *American Woman*, with guitarist Randy Bachman founding the crunch-driven Bachman-Turner Overdrive a few years later.

This new genre of rock would, in time, give Neil Bogart far greater success than anything he achieved during the Sixties.

Peter Criscoula kicked off the 1970s in fine style, marrying Lydia DiLeonardo on 31 January. He had proposed the previous May, manfully telling her that he had no intention of getting a job or paying for the wedding as he 'was going to single-mindedly pursue my musical career'. What woman wouldn't swoon at this charmer's silver-shrouded words? That boy should have been a fox instead of a cat. After a spring honeymoon in Spain and England – where the Criscoulas took in a show by rising star Elton John – it was back to the States and on to a new band, Chelsea.

Meanwhile, over in Washington Heights and midway through the year, Steve Coronel found himself playing a similar role to that of Ivan Vaughn, who, over a decade ago and an ocean away, introduced Paul McCartney to John Lennon. Steve had played with Stanley Eisen's post-Post War Baby Boom band Tree and had also been in the Long Island Sounds and Bullfrog Bheer with Gene Klein, and now here he was, introducing the two. Famously, it did not go well.

As Stanley recalled in his memoir, Klein was so arrogant he apparently thought only he and Lennon and McCartney could write original songs, so was taken aback when this kid three years younger than him ably demonstrated that he too could string some words and music together. Not surprisingly, this arrogance didn't sit well with Eisen, who resented being judged by a guy whose then-repertoire included gems such as 'My Uncle is a Raft' and, disturbingly, 'My Mother is the Most Beautiful Woman in the World'.

Despite this initial antipathy, they soon found themselves together in a band, where they soon realised they had much in common, such as their Jewish heritage, their tastes in music, their work ethic, and their drive to succeed. Mutual respect soon replaced the early distrust. Eisen and Klein fell into their future roles of rhythm guitar and bass, respectively, with both taking turns on lead vocals, and the band, called Rainbow, was completed by Coronel on lead guitar, Brooke Ostrander on keyboards, and Tony Zaralla behind the drum kit.

Paul Frehley, not yet fully transitioned to Ace, drifted through 1970 in a similar fashion to Peter Criscoula, minus the wedding. In other words, he played in a variety of bands hoping each was 'the one', while neatly sidestepping getting a job. Along the way, he attended the New York Pop Festival on 27 July, featuring Grand Funk Railroad, Jethro Tull, Steppenwolf, and others, but for Frehley, the main attraction was Jimi Hendrix. After blagging his way backstage, he was mistaken for a roadie and found himself setting up Mitch Mitchell's drum kit alongside the man himself. This festival date fell midway through Hendrix's Cry of Love tour, the guitarist's final tour, as he died later that year. August found Frehley at the Festival for Peace at Shea Stadium, where he similarly saw Janis Joplin play one of her last shows.

The dissolution of The Beatles and the loss of late-Sixties titans such as Hendrix, Joplin, and Jim Morrison the following year, was as much an indication of the shifting musical landscape as the emergence of hard rock and heavy metal. Early in 1971, another new music genre would be forged, one that would give the Seventies a distinctive identity, and that would have a lasting impact on the four musicians that would eventually coalesce as Kiss.

1971

On 24 March 1971, T. Rex made their second appearance on Britain's *Top of the Pops* to promote their single 'Hot Love', which was enjoying the first of a six-week run at number one. Just prior to taking the stage, Chelita Secunda, personal assistant to T. Rex frontman Marc Bolan, suggested she daub some glitter on his cheeks, just under his eyes. Bolan agreed and then went before thc cameras, destined to become the talk of the schoolyard and the workplace the day after transmission. That one performance signalled the birth of the decade's first superstar and its first musical phenomenon, glam rock. It is safe to say that the future members of Kiss did not see that show, but it was an influential pebble in the water and its ripples were already spreading.

'This fucking band is it! This is the band!' This is Peter Criscoula talking to his wife Lydia, via his autobiography *Makeup to Breakup*, about joining the band he knew was going to be his passport to success. But he wasn't talking about Kiss, which was still two years distant. The band in question was Chelsea.

This five-piece consisted of Peter Shepley (vocals), Mike Brand (guitar), Chris Aridas (guitar), Michael Benvenga (bass and vocals) and the newly christened Peter Cris on drums (The second 'S' was added later, but from here on in he will be referred to as Peter Criss). They were signed to Decca and their eponymous debut was produced by Lewis Merenstein, best known for his work on Van Morrison's *Astral Weeks* (1968). The album's credentials are further boosted by the presence of former Velvet Underground member John Cale, who provided the viola solos on two of the tracks.

It doesn't hurt that there are also some potentially good songs – 'Let's Call It a Day' has a proggy, English pastoral vibe *a la* The Moody Blues – but unfortunately, the arrangements are cluttered, too much of it sounding like it was written by people that *did* go to San Francisco and put some flowers in their hair. Criss's only writing credit is on the band composition 'Polly Von'. The album flopped, various members left, and, to paraphrase, this fucking band wasn't it.

A late-in-the-day addition to the Chelsea line-up was guitarist Stan Penridge, and in August, he, Criss, and bassist Benvenga ditched the Chelsea moniker and rebranded themselves as Lips. After rehearsing for a couple of months, Lips played their first live gig in October.

The Haight-Ashbury scene was also a clear influence on Molimo, their brand of psychedelic folk especially indebted to Jefferson Airplane.

The band, a six-piece, was named after a horn-like trumpet used by the Mbuti pygmy tribes of the Democratic Republic of Congo, and consisted of Christine Murphy (vocals), Tom Ellis (vocals and guitar), Roy Singer (keyboards), Barry Dempsey (bass), Dave Polinski (drums) and one Paul Frehley on guitar. The sextet didn't get as far as recording an album, but they did record a three-track demo for RCA before the record company bailed. This acetate was lost until 2014 when it was rediscovered in a barn in upstate New York and is now available to hear on YouTube.

Frehley quit Molimo after RCA pulled the plug – it was during his time with them that 'Ace' became his stage name – but remained friends with its members. When Murphy, Ellis and Singer later formed a new band, Tomorrow Morning, it was possibly no coincidence that 'Freewheeling', their 1974-and-only single, was released on Casablanca Records and produced by Kenny Kerner and Richie Wise, who had produced Kiss's debut album, released earlier that year on Casablanca.

Rainbow, meanwhile, carried on gigging, playing the likes of 'Locomotive Breath' by Jethro Tull, 'When You Dance' by Neil Young, and Free's 'All Right Now', interspersed with some Stanley and Simmons originals. In April, on hearing of another band called Rainbow, they changed their name to Wicked Lester, and played their first gig at the Rivoli Theatre, South Fallsberg, NY. A second show, in Atlantic City, would be their last live appearance.

On the plus side, Eisen's determination got them a production deal with Electric Lady Studio head Ron Johnsen, who gave them the green light to record an album while he shipped around for a record contract. Several auditions later, Epic Records were willing to sign the band, providing they got rid of lead guitarist Stephen Coronel. Klein had been Coronel's friend since their early teens, so delivering the bad news fell to him. This moment was a milestone of sorts, as it demonstrated Eisen and Klein's determination. They were in a band to be successful, not just to knock about with their mates. The recruitment of replacement guitarist Ron Leejack, who had played slide guitar on the Cactus album *Restrictions*, was one of the factors that contributed to the recording of the Wicked Lester album lumbering on into 1972.

Stephen Coronel would receive a cowriting credit and royalties for 'Goin' Blind' on *Hotter Than Hell* (1974) and 'She' on *Dressed to Kill* (1975). He dropped off the radar until his arrest in 2014 on child pornography charges and was sentenced to ten years in prison two years later. He was released on parole in 2019.

1972

The glam rock fire begun by Marc Bolan in 1971 blazed brightest in 1972. David Bowie saw his career hit stratospheric heights when he adopted the persona of alien visitor Ziggy Stardust and released the single 'Starman'. The moment the shock-haired carrot-top limply drapes his arm around Mick Ronson's shoulder during his 6 July *Top of the Pops* appearance is as iconic and revolutionary as Bolan's glitter tears the year before.

Wolverhampton rockers Slade, who entered the '70s as skinheads, grew their hair and nailed their colours to the glam mast. By the end of 1971, 'Coz I Luv You' earned them their first UK number one, and for the first half of the decade they were the colossus of the UK singles chart, outperforming all rivals, including T. Rex and Bowie. Slade were harder rocking than many of their contemporaries, as were Mott the Hoople, a band on the verge of splitting until they enjoyed massive success with the Bowie-penned 'All the Young Dudes', which spurred them on to make three essential albums and a clutch of hit singles. Others to score big in Britain included art school combo Roxy Music and thrice-round-the-block bandwagon-jumper Gary Glitter (nee Paul Gadd), who would tread the same depraved paths as Steve Coronel.

Glam was less ubiquitous across the pond, where its US identity as 'glitter rock' perhaps posited it too close to the disposability of bubblegum. The genre's undisputed titan was Alice Cooper, a group that had flirted with psychedelia and hard rock before creating their unique gold lamé Grand Guignol take on glam. Their album *School's Out* and its title single broke them worldwide in '72, and their attendant stage show introduced a level of theatricality unseen in rock. Meanwhile, Lou Reed was another surprising recipient of David Bowie's patronage, who, along with Mick Ronson, propelled the former Velvet Underground main man's *Transformer* album to mainstream success. Such success would forever elude the New York Dolls, who made their live debut on Christmas Eve 1971, but their proto-punk brand of glam burlesque would have a profound impact that belied their poor sales. Interestingly, Peter Criss would unsuccessfully audition for the band following the November 1972 death of original drummer Billy Murcia, but it would be his old friend Jerry Nolan who got the gig.

All the above glammy goings-on would influence the nascent Kiss, none more so than the Dolls, the Cooper group, and Slade.

Around this time Stanley Eisen decided he didn't want to be Stanley Eisen anymore. It wasn't 'rock star' enough. So, he shunted his first name to last, and adopted 'Paul', reasoning that, with the likes of Paul McCartney and Paul Rodgers, it already had a proven rock pedigree. Gene Klein also decided it was time to try on a new name, so switched to Gene Simmons, a name chosen randomly and not as a play on that of British-born Hollywood actress Jean Simmons.

It was under these new identities that Stanley and Simmons got their first recording credit when they supplied backing vocals to two songs on singer Lyn Christopher's first and only album. According to Christopher's website, an uncredited Peter Criss also provided hand claps on one of these songs. The album was produced by Ron Johnsen, who coincidentally also produced the *Chelsea* album and was currently occupying the control booth for Wicked Lester.

Unfortunately, Wicked Lester failed to attract a record label, so their album was consigned to the vaults, occasionally surfacing in bootleg form, until three of its tracks, 'Keep Me Waiting', 'Love Her All I Can', and 'She' saw official release on the 2001 Kiss *Box Set*. Not only were record companies unimpressed by the Wicked Lester sessions, Stanley and Simmons also found themselves quite indifferent to the fruits of their labours. As far as they could hear, there was no uniformity to the music, nothing that made it sound like the same band on all songs, and there was none of the guitar-driven hard rock that both men were gravitating towards with new compositions such as 'Strutter' and 'Deuce'. Their solution was to quit Wicked Lester and form the band they wanted to be, and the stars started to align with this ad, placed in the 31 August edition of *Rolling Stone*: 'EXPD. ROCK & roll drummer looking for orig. grp. doing soft & hard music. Peter, Brooklyn'.

In an oft-told tale, Simmons phoned Criss while a party was going on at the latter's house, and Gene's line of questioning quickly established that image was as important as musical ability. How tall are you? Are you fat? Do you have long hair? Are you good-looking? Would you be willing to dress in drag? Criss turned the interview into an impromptu party game and asked his guests to answer the questions, all of whom responded in the affirmative.

Criss then met up for a face-to-face with Stanley and Simmons at Electric Lady, and they went to see him play at some Brooklyn mafia joint called the King's Lounge, so they could gauge his proficiency. When Criss stepped up to the mic to sing Wilson Pickett's 'The Midnight Hour', they knew they had their man.

After a couple of months of rehearsing, the trio played an unsuccessful showcase for Don Ellis, the head of Epic Records. The band, still using the Wicked Lester moniker, cranked up the volume, and the resultant monolithic cacophony soon sent Ellis scurrying from the room. In terms of progressing in the industry, it was a bust; in terms of progressing with their vision of being the band they wanted to see, it was significant, as it was the first time they wore white face paint. The distinctive characters hadn't yet arrived, but their gestation period had begun.

The band had initially toyed with being a power trio but jettisoned this idea in favour of filling out their sound. An ad seeking a lead guitarist 'with flash and ability' duly appeared in an early December issue of *The Village Voice*, which led to another audition that gained mythic proportions within the Kiss story.

1973

3 January. Or maybe it is late December. Like so much of Kiss's history, it all depends on who is telling the tale. Over thirty people responded to the ad, most of whom were no-hopers. The best so far was Bob Kulick, but while he had the guitar chops, he didn't have 'the look'. It was while they were auditioning him that a rather distinctive individual walked into their rehearsal loft. He 'stumbled and tripped. He was a real klutz', remembered Bobby McAdams, a friend of said individual, in *Nothin' to Lose*, the oral biography of Kiss's early years. He was 'kind of goofy and pigeon-toed', and 'moved in a rubbery way', recalled Stanley in his autobiography. And what everyone remembers is that he had two different coloured sneakers on, one red and one orange. And that he got everyone's hackles up when he let rip on his guitar while the band were still chatting to Kulick.

The odds were against this ill-mannered, poorly coordinated weirdo that couldn't even match his shoes, but when he launched into his solo during a run-through of 'Deuce', he annihilated the competition. But still, there was uncertainty. According to Criss, Stanley and Simmons' main reservation was the fact that Frehley was Chinese, while Criss tried to placate them, assuring them he was Mongolian. Frehley, meanwhile, claimed he was from another planet. He was none of these things, of course, but being of German descent with just a smidgen of Cherokee thrown in was apparently enough to make him one unusual looking fella. After a second audition, Paul Frehley was in. There was only one slight hiccup; there couldn't be two Pauls in the band. "No problem,' the newly appointed lead guitarist responded. 'Call me by my nickname. It's Ace'. The band was now complete.

The first order of business was to christen the band, and Stanley, on hearing that Criss's previous outfit had been called Lips, suggested Kiss, which got everyone's thumbs up. Next to be considered was the look. At first, they opted for the androgynous style sported by the New York Dolls, but whereas the Dolls could pull it off, Kiss looked, according to Stanley, 'like a bunch of firemen in drag'. They soon settled on black leather with silver highlights as their uniform, but as they couldn't afford the clothes they saw in the window of Jumpin' Jack Flash, they bought similar fabrics and designed their own. Stanley sewed a pair of black satin pants for both himself and Simmons; Frehley's early outfits were stitched together by his mother; Criss's mum smeared a pair of Hush Puppies in glue and then covered them in glitter; and Lydia Criscoula and her sister pitched in, creating t-shirts with a homemade, sparkly Kiss logo. Even that was homespun, drafted by Ace and refined by Paul. Accessories came from pet shops and S&M stores. The future multi-million-dollar brand essentially began as a cottage industry.

The Beatles were an inspiration insofar as Kiss wanted to emulate their model of no lead singer and no standalone frontman, but it was only after attending an Alice Cooper concert that the notion of creating four distinct characters, each with a unique facial design, took hold. Simmons indulged his love of monster movies and comic books and created a look that, according to his autobiography, crossed Godzilla with the Marvel comics character Black Bolt (or a Phantom of the Opera / Batman hybrid, according to his account in *Nothin' to Lose*); Stanley placed a single black star over his right eye, a symbol of his ambition; Criss adopted a feline look because he considered cats to be tough and independent, which was how he saw himself; and Frehley, who was already telling anybody that would listen that he was from the planet Jendell, became the band's resident alien.

However, it would be some months before these embryonic designs resembled their iconic versions. For example, in an early photo showing the band with Sid Benjamin, owner of The Daisy club in Amityville that they would play a dozen times in 1973, the black patterns around Simmons' eyes are little more than amorphous inkblots, Frehley has forgotten the whiteface, and the cartoonish look of shocked surprise on Criss's cat face suggests he may just have fallen victim to a five-fingered rectal invasion. Stanley, meanwhile, has neither his trademark black star nor white face, settling for mascara that looks like it was applied whilst wearing boxing gloves.

Kiss made their live debut on Tuesday, 30 January 1973, at the Coventry Hotel in Queens, playing two sets to an audience which Stanley remembers being 'less than ten.' Simmons, however, narrows it down to 'Lydia Criss, a girl named Jan who I was seeing, and Jan's friend', so Stanley's recollection, while not incorrect, might just be the earliest and oddest example of the mighty Kiss hyperbole machine in action. Either way, it was an inauspicious start for the future Hottest Band in the Land, and they were booked for the Wednesday and Thursday as well.

On 9 March, they made their first appearance at the Daisy, with Sid Benjamin initially sceptical about this new act he had booked. The scepticism turned to outrage when he saw that his customers weren't drinking but standing slack-jawed looking at the stage. To compound matters, Simmons would go into the audience, take the drink from their hands, put it on the table, and encourage them to clap. Meanwhile, the club's fearsome bouncer thought they were 'a transvestite band' and threatened to kill them. Both bouncer and Benjamin were soon won over, the former by the band's no-frills rock and roll and the latter by the fact that, as word got out, the number of people attending the Kiss shows soon exceeded his club's 144 capacity. By the time they played the last of their dozen shows at the Daisy, on 25 August, Kiss had outgrown the club.

On Friday, 10 August, a fortnight before their final Daisy gig, the band played a show at the Hotel Diplomat that was of considerably greater consequence. The Diplomat was still an operational hotel, but its glory days were long past. Bobby McAdams, a friend of Frehley's, described it as 'a dump', and Binky Philips of The Planets, who had previously played the Diplomat with Kiss, said it was 'basically a flophouse – very run-down and sleazy, a notch above skid row'. But the New York Dolls had played there, and that put it on the map for all the other bands that comprised the New York 'street scene' that Kiss were both a part of and apart from.

Kiss hired the hotel's second-floor Crystal Room, a dilapidated ballroom, and, recognising that they could never fill it on their own, also paid two other bands from that 'street scene', Street Punk and Luger, both of whom had larger followings than Kiss, to share the bill. They then took out press ads and littered the city with flyers which suggested Kiss were the headliners. However, as part of their 'contract' with the other bands, they took the middle slot, going on stage at nine-thirty, not-so-coincidentally the time they had put on the homemade press kit they had mailed out to industry executives. Finally, they then packed the front rows with friends and family wearing Kiss t-shirts that Peter and Paul had made the previous night.

The number of movers and shakers that attended the Diplomat that night is unknown, but one was enough when that individual happened to be Bill Aucoin. A television producer/director who had previously worked on the original *Supermarket Sweep* gameshow, Aucoin was currently involved in a show called *Flip Slide*, which took the viewer into the recording studio with acts such as John Lennon and Yoko Ono, The Raspberries, Roberta Flack, Judy Collins, and Blood, Sweat & Tears. Aucoin cornered Simmons after Kiss's set and announced that he would like to manage the band, promising to get them a recording contract within thirty days. It was an audacious proposition, but it turned out Bill knew a guy.

Re-enter Neil Bogart, late of Buddah Records. The Ohio Express had reached the end of the line, the 1910 Fruitgum Company had closed shop, and the bubblegum fad had burst, as bubbles are wont to do. Bogart had just launched his own label, Casablanca, and was looking for his first signing. Bill Aucoin, who had shone the *Flip Side* spotlight on some of Bogart's previous acts, passed a Kiss demo tape onto him a week after he had seen the band at the Diplomat, and Bogart, in turn, handed it over to Kenny Kerner, who that year had produced the chart-topping single by Stories, 'Brother Louie'. Kerner liked what he heard and told Bogart as much. A few days later, Bogart, Kerner, Casablanca vice-president Larry Harris, Aucoin, Aucoin's business partner Joyce Biawitz and a few others attended a Kiss showcase at the Henry Letang School of Dance in Manhattan.

In his book *And Party Every Day: The Inside Story of Casablanca Records*, Harris describes this incongruous venue as a space 'typically used for the kind of dance rehearsals and recitals attended by the moms and pops of the performers'.

Kiss took the stage – 'four seven-foot monsters in eight-inch platforms' according to Harris – and ran through a set list of less than half a dozen songs, including future favourites 'Strutter' and 'Deuce'. The show had none of the special effects later made famous by the band, and, again, by Harris's account, 'the makeup was cheap. The whiteface was more like powder than grease paint. It was pale and transparent rather than stark… It ran off their cheeks as they began to sweat'. But their visual and sonic ferocity made an impression, and a deal was struck on 1 November. Kiss now had a manager and record label.

That same month, the band entered Bell Studios to record their debut album and worked with various people within Aucoin's Rock Steady organisation and Casablanca to improve their stage craft. A primary contributor was Sean Delaney, Aucoin's boyfriend, who Criss credits as being the fifth member of Kiss. He had the band dye their hair the same colour of blueish black and would choreograph their stage moves, videotaping their rehearsals so they could see what worked and what didn't. Many of these moves, such as the three guitarists swaying in unison during 'Deuce' or swapping positions on stage, remain in their show today. Meanwhile, it was Harris, a big Who fan, who advocated the smashing of a guitar at the conclusion of each show, while Bogart suggested the levitating drum kit, and brought in a magician to teach Simmons how to spit fire.

The fire-breathing made its stage debut at Kiss's most prestigious gig to date, a New Year's Eve concert at the New York Academy of Music. At first glance it didn't look like a particularly promising outing for the band, as they were a last-minute addition to the line-up, so didn't feature in the show's advertising, and they were fourth on the bill after the Blue Oyster Cult, Iggy Pop & the Stooges, and Teenage Lust. Then, disaster struck during their set, not once but twice. The first instance could have ended Kiss's career there and then, and involved miniature hand-held flash bombs that Simmons would throw into the air above the audience, where they would explode spectacularly but harmlessly. That was the plan. The reality was that he accidentally threw his first one into the face of a fan who was standing on his seat, and the resultant explosion sent the young man sprawling. In *Nothin' to Lose*, the oral biography of Kiss's early years, it is clear this unfortunate individual was truly injured in the incident; Stanley recalls 'blisters on his face' and Simmons describes it more colourfully, saying that it looked like 'cheese had melted over the left side of his face. He looked like someone from a Hammer horror movie'. Incredibly, no litigation was forthcoming. The victim simply thought the band were 'awesome' and that 'that was the coolest show I've ever seen'. As he was helped into the ambulance, photographer Bob Gruen recalls the kid telling a reporter that Kiss was his favourite band. Hand-thrown flash bombs were quietly dropped from the act.

The second incident involved Simmons again, and this time the wound was self-inflicted when his hair was set ablaze during his fire-breathing stunt. Although the bassist was unaware of what he had done, a stunned band and audience looked on slack-jawed, and Bill Aucoin's face presumably adopted the hue that Procol Harum sang about for the second time that evening. Fortunately, a quick-thinking Sean Delaney bounded on stage and extinguished the fire with a wet towel, meaning that the worst Simmons suffered was some smudged makeup and an asymmetrical haircut. Despite this, the fire-breathing remained part of the act, becoming Simmons' signature move and an expected part of every Kiss concert.

Also making its debut at the Academy of Music gig was the KISS sign, an innovation of Aucoin's, which, although it has evolved with technology, also remains a staple of any Kiss show.

What made the Academy show so important was it got the band noticed. For starters, they were now playing to a crowd of over 4,000, probably more than the rest of their 1973 shows put together. It got them their greatest press coverage to date, even bagging them an appearance in the

UK's *Sounds* music newspaper. And, now that they were sharing the stage with actual recording artists such as Blue Oyster Cult and Iggy Pop, it got them noticed by their peers. Interviewed for *Nothin' to Lose*, BOC's Eric Bloom admits to watching the band from the side of the stage and being 'blown away'. Bandmate Buck Dharma thought, 'the sheer spectacle of Kiss was amazing'. Stooges drummer Scott Asheton conceded while 'Iggy could be outrageous on stage, it was nothing compared to Kiss'. Dee Dee Ramone, in the audience that night, thought Kiss stole the show. Harold C. Black, multi-instrumentalist with Teenage Lust, voiced the problem that was to vex many of Kiss's future headliners: 'What the hell can we do to top this?'

1974 – Kiss and Hotter Than Hell

Kiss

Personnel:
Paul Stanley: rhythm guitar, vocals
Ace Frehley: lead guitar, vocals
Gene Simmons: bass, vocals
Peter Criss: drums, vocals
Additional personnel:
Eddie Solon, Marc Labow, and Richie Wise: 'Firehouse' fire engine
Bruce Foster: piano
Bobby: handclaps on 'Nothin' to Lose'
Recorded at Bell Sound Studios, New York City, October 1973
Produced by Kenny Kerner and Richie Wise
Released: 18 February 1974
Running time: 35.07
Highest chart place: US: 87
Tracklisting: 1. 'Strutter' (Stanley, Simmons) 3.10, 2. 'Nothin' to Lose' (Simmons) 3.26, 3. 'Firehouse' (Stanley) 3.18, 4. 'Cold Gin' (Frehley) 4.21, 5. 'Let Me Know' (Stanley) 2.58, 6. 'Kissin' Time' (Mann, Lowe) 3.52, 7. 'Deuce' (Simmons) 3.05, 8. 'Love Theme from Kiss' (Stanley, Simmons, Criss, Frehley) 2.24, 9. '100,000 Years' (Stanley, Simmons) 3.22, 10. 'Black Diamond' (Stanley) 5.11

Hotter Than Hell

Personnel:
Paul Stanley: rhythm guitar, vocals
Ace Frehley: lead guitar, vocals
Gene Simmons: bass, vocals
Peter Criss: drums, vocals
Recorded at the Village Recorder, Los Angeles, August 1974
Produced by Kenny Kerner and Richie Wise
Released: 22 October 1974
Running time: 33.02
Highest chart place: US: 100
Tracklisting: 1. 'Got to Choose' (Stanley) 3.54, 2. 'Parasite' (Frehley) 3.01, 3. 'Goin' Blind' (Simmons, Coronel) 3.36, 4. 'Hotter Than Hell' (Stanley) 3.31, 5. 'Let Me Go, Rock and Roll' (Simmons, Stanley) 2.14, 6 'All the Way' (Simmons) 3.18, 7. 'Watchin' You' (Simmons) 3.43, 8. 'Mainline' (Stanley) 3.50, 9. 'Comin' Home' (Frehley, Stanley) 2.37, 10 'Strange Ways' (Frehley) 3.18

The new year started with a minor identity crisis for Paul Stanley. Neil Bogart decided that Stanley's single eye star was too effeminate and suggested the singer change it. He also expressed concern about Stanley's on-stage mincing and prancing, believing that any whiff of sexual ambiguity could spell the end of any aspiring mid-Seventies hard rock band. Stanley took one for the team and adopted a design that looked like a wide-eyed Zorro mask; later accounts variously describe this look as the 'bandit' or the 'raccoon'. The rhythm guitarist sported this makeup at the band's press launch at the Fillmore East on 8 January.

A month later, by the time the band played Casablanca's launch party in Los Angeles in February, the star was back. The 'bandit' never fitted Stanley's personality, and, despite Bogart's misgivings, the singer was entirely comfortable with the androgynous role he had adopted. Besides, one of the biggest bands of the early '70s had a male lead singer called Alice. Speaking of which, the artist formerly known as Vincent Furnier attended the Casablanca party, where, when asked about Kiss, he famously quipped, 'What these guys need is a gimmick'.

Stanley's cosmetic 'identity crisis' aside, 1974 got off to a flying start for Kiss. On 5 February, they began their first jaunt around North America, beginning in Edmonton in Canada and set to culminate nine months later in Houston, Texas. Headlining intermittently, they usually served as mismatched support for bluesy Brits Savoy Brown and folk-proggies Renaissance, amongst others. On 17 February, Kiss were booed off stage in Long Beach, CA, where they were bottom of another brilliantly disharmonious bill headlined by Rory Gallagher and featuring Fleetwood Mac and Tim Buckley. To compound their ignominy, the Fleetwood Mac in question was the infamous fake version of the band, who miraculously escaped the crowd's wrath. There was the occasional compatible pairing when the band shared the stage with the likes of the Dolls, Blue Oyster Cult, and future rivals Aerosmith.

On 18 February, the band's eponymous debut hit record shops. The cover was shot by Joel Brodsky, a prolific rock photographer whose most famous photograph is arguably the 'young lion' shot of Jim Morrison. He shot several of the Doors album covers, including their debut, as well as the iconic covers of Isaac Hayes' *Black Moses* and Funkadelic's *Maggot Brain*. For the *Kiss* cover, he did a simple *With the Beatles*-type shot of the band's faces. Simmons and Stanley have both claimed Brodsky saw their makeup, assumed they were clowns, and offered to get red noses and balloons. It's a good story, but perhaps too good to be true. Brodsky has dismissed this version of events as the product of overactive imaginations, and a quick peek at his similar cover for the 1968 debut album by Nazz suggests he knew what he was doing.

The album opens with 'Strutter', a glam classic that reflected Stanley's 'ongoing fascination with women in the New York glitter scene'. Criss's drum intro sets the ball rolling before Stanley punches out some power chords that set out the band's stall as 'a kick-ass, balls-out, full-tilt, volume-heavy rock 'n' roll' band', as he described Kiss to *Classic Rock* in 2021. He neglected to mention their apparent fondness for hyphens. Simmons provides Stones-y swagger, and Frehley leaves no string unbent in his two short but exhilarating solos. It is Stanley's vocals that seal the deal, however. Raspy, seductive, and oddly heartfelt, they owe more to the Ronettes than Mick 'n' Keith and co. 'Strutter' demonstrates Stanley's pop sensibilities and ear for a catchy tune, but Simmons gets a cowrite credit as the star bearer modelled elements of his song on an earlier Simmons piece entitled 'Stanley the Parrot'. A 1970 demo of this can be found on YouTube and lacks the, well, strut of Stanley's composition, resembling instead some pastoral, acid-folk band like Dr. Strangely Strange.

'Strutter' was the third and final single released from *Kiss* and was as unsuccessful as its predecessors.

The second cut is 'Nothin' to Lose', another fast rocker that shows that Simmons, too, knew his way around a catchy tune. The bassist opts to shout his vocal, which works well enough in the context of the song, but it buries his otherwise melodic, occasionally McCartney-esque singing style that might have served the song better. As it stands, it is the scat from the Cat, Criss's soulful, throaty, ad-libbing over the chorus, that enlivens the number, as do guest player Bruce Foster's glammy glissando *a la* T. Rex's 'Get It On', and the echo-drenched hand clapping. It was released simultaneously with the parent album and is surely the first and only debut 45 to celebrate the joys of anal sex. Industry magazine *Cash Box* were fans, calling it 'a very heavy, very tasty rocker reminiscent of Deep Purple… Look out for this band, they will happen, and big, in the coming weeks'. Ultimately, it proved incapable of troubling a chart populated by Terry Jacks, Barbara Streisand, and Jim Stafford (who, it will be remembered, did not like spiders and snakes), and it took considerably longer than 'the coming weeks' for the band to 'happen'.

While 'Strutter' nodded vaguely in the general direction of the Rolling Stones, Stanley made no bones about which English band, and song, served as the inspiration for 'Firehouse'. Interviewed for the official Kiss biography *Behind the Mask*, the singer said he was so enamoured of 'Fire Brigade' by The Move that 'I stole it and rewrote it'. Well, not quite. 'Firehouse' is considerably more leaden than Roy Wood's psychedelia-dusted pop classic, and the former's seemingly endless 'whoo-whoo-whoos' smack too much of forced excitement. It was also an undeniable dip when compared to its two predecessors on *Kiss*. It did, however, become a live favourite, featuring wailing crimson crank sirens and Gene Simmons' fire-spewing party trick.

'Cold Gin' marks Ace Frehley's recorded debut as a songwriter, and perhaps unsurprisingly for a guitarist with a fondness for the booze, it was a song about a fondness for the booze. Equally unsurprisingly, it is a heavy riff-fest with lots of space for frittery guitar embellishments. At the time it was recorded, Frehley didn't have the confidence to sing lead, so that duty fell, famously and ironically, to Simmons, the band's only lifelong teetotaller. 'Cold Gin' remained in the setlist even during the Frehley-free, bare-faced years, and when Ace rejoined the band in 1996, he and Simmons shared lead vocals. Fun fact: Tommy Thayer, who would take over the Spaceman role in the twenty-first century, was once in a Kiss tribute band called Cold Gin.

'Let Me Know' is the song Stanley played when first introduced to Simmons, although at that time it was called 'Sunday Driver', a phrase found in the opening line. Simmons and Stanley share lead vocals on this fifties-based rock and roller, and its sweet 'boy wants to meet girl' lyrics wouldn't have sounded out of place a couple of decades earlier. An instrumental coda takes the song off in a new direction and threatens to jazz things up before an indecently hasty fade puts the song to bed.

'Deuce' opens side two of the original album release, although later editions would have an extra song added, as we shall see. An R&B song given a hard rock makeover, it was another early track indebted to Jagger and company and remains one of Simmons' best compositions. The bassist growls and shouts his way through lyrics which even he admits are meaningless, and six songs into the album his unique approach to singing is now already well and truly established. 'Deuce' was Frehley's audition piece for the band, and his wailing, off-kilter, and thoroughly thrilling soloing throughout make it clear why he got the job. The song served as the band's show-starter up until the *Destroyer* tour, and then appeared only intermittently before regaining pole position during the *Alive/Worldwide* tour of 1996 and '97.

The next track, 'Love Theme from Kiss', remains one of the most unusual entries in the band's catalogue, being the only track cowritten by all four members of the original lineup, and the only instrumental recorded by them (Frehley would dabble in instrumentals in his solo work, but Kiss would not revisit the format until their disastrous 1981 concept album *Music From 'The Elder'*). Equally unusually, the tune has a certain funkiness to it, albeit one more in keeping with the theme to a Quinn Martin production than future labelmates Parliament/Funkadelic. 'Love Theme from Kiss' hasn't got a lot to say, no pun intended, and hits the fade around the two-minute mark.

The penultimate track '100,000 Years', is a Stanley and Simmons co-write about an astronaut returning to Earth millennia after his departure and a lyrical space oddity in the Kiss canon. It may not be as accomplished as later songs exploring similar territory – Queen's '39', Hawkwind's 'Spirit of the Age' – but, along with the likes of 'Cold Gin' and 'Black Diamond', it shows that the young pup version of the band was far more lyrically adventurous than all later models, who plucked only 'I Wanna Fuck You' and 'You Wanna Fuck Me' songs from their jotter. The song opens with a rumbling bass, includes a mini drum solo from Criss and some furious arpeggios from Frehley, and this showcasing of individual talents would be fully exploited when '100,000 Years' was played live.

'Black Diamond' provides a satisfying album closer. Almost. A song in four parts, it opens with an acoustic ballad sung by Stanley before Criss takes over the vocals for part two's rock 'n' soul hybrid. The third section is instrumental, the melody shifting gear to three-four time, while Frehley solos away wildly. So far, all good, but the wheel comes off the bus in part four, a series of increasingly distorted and slowed-down A chords that start off thuddingly dull and go downhill from there. Incredibly, this section is given the lion's share of the running time, approximately two-fifths, an astonishing creative decision when all three preceding parts are far more melodic and inventive, and each more worthy of the expanded time accorded part four.

This, however, was a minor blip compared to the album's biggest flaw. On the one hand, the production is arguably the cleanest Kiss ever had; Simmons' bass, for example, would never have such clarity again. But ultimately, it was a botched job, one that failed to put the power into pop and the hard into rock. This is particularly surprising as the men in the control booth were Richie Wise and Kenny Kerner, who had previously been singer/guitarist and lyricist/producer respectively with Dust, who had released two of the heaviest albums of the early '70s. It didn't hurt that their drummer was Marc Bell, later of Richard Hell and The Voidoids and, as Marky Ramone, the Ramones. Wise and Kerner had somehow lost the power they had brought to their own albums, leaving *Kiss* as tinny as a transistor radio listened to under clandestine covers.

Sales for the album were disappointing, reported variously as between 60,000 and 75,000 units. This could simply be down to Kiss being an unknown act with zero radio support and no touring experience to speak of, but perhaps it was also a case of bad timing. The New York Dolls were about to disappear for a thirty-year hiatus, Alice had taken off the makeup for the cover shoot of 1973's *Muscle of Love*, and Bowie had broken up the Spiders from Mars and was about to release *Diamond Dogs*, his final glam album. As far back as June '73, Marc Bolan had told *Melody Maker* that glam rock was dead. Yet here was this new band who, with their greasepaint and Cooper eyes and silver hair, looked for all the world like they were standing on the dock after the *SS Glam* had sailed.

The *Kiss* story is one that has a happy ending. The album's sales were jumpstarted following the success of *Alive!* and it was eventually certified gold. Its songs have stood the test of time, with many becoming enduring 'Kiss klassiks', four of which featured in the band's three-year *End of the Road* tour (2019-2022), purportedly their last ever.

On 21 February, the band made their television debut on Dick Clark's *In Concert* programme. Their three-song set – 'Nothin' to Lose', 'Firehouse', and 'Black Diamond' – was broadcast on 29 March, coincidentally the day of their second television outing on *The Mike Douglas Show*. This show included a short interview, and Simmons stepped up to bat after the other members got cold feet. It was an unmitigated disaster, as 'The Demon' got caught up in playing the part, gurning, and grimacing throughout like Bela Lugosi on speed. He tried to pass himself off as 'evil incarnate', but fellow guest Totie Fields easily got the better of him, quipping, 'Incidentally, he's up for adoption' and asking, 'Wouldn't it be funny if under this he was just a nice Jewish boy?' Simmons might not have gotten much of a reaction from the studio audience, but he elicited a furious one from his bandmates for promoting himself rather than the band, the album, or the tour. The ego had landed.

By now, sales of *Kiss* had levelled out, so to give it a further boost Neil Bogart came up with an idea straight out of the Fifties, a national kissing contest. He asked the band to cover the 1959 Bobby Rydell hit 'Kissin' Time' to promote the contest, which they agreed to do only if Bogart promised not to release it as a single or slap it on any future album. Naturally, Mr Casablanca consented, but when the band had finished in the studio, he promptly released it as a single. Not only that, when *Kiss* went to re-pressing in July, it had strangely sprouted an additional track. 'Kissin' Time' is no disgrace, however. It successfully updates an old chestnut for the glam era, provides the three lead singers a verse each, and features a shouty intro that predicts the Bowie-Jagger cover of 'Dancing in the Street' over a decade later. It also bagged them their first placing on the US singles charts, even if it was a lowly 83.

Meanwhile, the tour trundled on. Of note is their gig at the Centennial Hall in London, Ontario, on 25 July, where Rush served as the opening act for the first time. The Canadian trio would open for Kiss many times over the next couple of years, but this would be the only occasion original drummer John Rutsey occupied the drum stool. Kiss only played a couple of shows in August, spending most of the month recording their sophomore album at the Village Recorder in Los Angeles, and then it was out on the road again for a clutch of dates in September. Roy Wood and his then-current band Wizzard provided support for one date on 28 September, a fact that must have delighted Stanley, a massive fan of Wood's earlier band, the Move. Unfortunately, the Detroit audience didn't share the Starchild's passion, and Wizzard were booed throughout their set.

Hotter Than Hell hit the shelves on 22 October, a mere eight months after the debut, and sported an eye-popping Japanese-themed cover. This was the brainchild of the South African-born photographer Norman Seeff, who had immigrated to the States in 1969 and was making a name for himself with his work on the Band's *Stage Fright* album, and as art director on *Exile on Main Street* by the Rolling Stones. Seeff was inspired by the work of Tadanori Yokoo, whom he had recently met in Japan. 'I think the way Kiss were dressed and who they were suggested to me that Yokoo's work would be an ideal direction for them. As we went further, I thought, 'Why not put the title in Japanese as well?' I called in a brilliant designer, John Van Hamersveld, to do the design.' Simmons credits the cover with helping break the band in Japan: 'The result of that was the Japanese instantly took to the band. We started reading cover stories about the band. The Japanese thought we had taken the makeup from Japanese Kabuki theatre'. Frehley's image on the cover was the subject of much doctoring. The guitarist had injured himself in a car crash and could only apply makeup to half his face; the rest was airbrushed in. The Japanese spelling of his surname is also incorrect and translates as 'Fury'.

'Got to Choose' is the album opener, and here songwriter Stanley chooses the riff from Boomerang's version of the Wilson Picket song 'Ninety-Nine and a Half (Won't Do)', but the melody is sufficiently far removed from its inspiration as 'Firehouse' was from 'Fire Brigade'. 'Got to Choose' is also as good a candidate as any to support Simmons' oft-stated claim that Kiss strove to be a 'hard rock Beatles'.

Ace Frehley's 1978 solo outing suggested to many that he was the hardest rocking of the band, but the evidence was there as early as 'Parasite', a speed metal song before the term was coined. As with 'Cold Gin', Simmons adopts lead vocal duties, but the standout here is Criss, who maintains a jazzy shuffle throughout the verses before dovetailing perfectly with Ace during the latter's solo. Frehley revisited the song on his 2016 covers album *Origins Vol. 1*.

The third track is 'Goin' Blind', written by Simmons and Stephen Coronel. According to Coronel, talking to Legendary Rock Interviews, the inspiration for this was Mountain's 'Theme from an Imaginary Western': 'I wanted… That type of big rolling chord progression'. It is an epic tune, with Simmons investing in the vocal rather than shouting, and has a wonderfully atypical Frehley solo. Unfortunately, the song's lyric about a 93-year-old man having a relationship with a sixteen-year-old girl has always creeped this reviewer out, and this from someone born in a nation that tried to convince television viewers that young women were attracted to Reg Varney and Bob Grant (non-British readers might need to Google this one). Surprisingly, this age-inappropriate line came from Stanley and not the leery Simmons.

Stanley's title track is up next, with his most blatant 'homage' to date. 'Hotter Than Hell' is suitably scorching, but who can listen to it and not hear Free's 'All Right Now'?

As with *Kiss*, the band close side one with a fast-paced song whose roots stretch back to rock's first decade. A Stanley-Simmons composition, 'Let Me Go, Rock and Roll' was the only single released from *Hotter Than Hell*, but it went nowhere despite the rock and roll revivalism prompted by the box-office success of *American Graffiti* (1973) and the television series *Happy Days*, which first aired in the summer of '74.

Side two opens with 'All the Way,' an irresistibly catchy Simmons song that crisscrosses the state line between hard rock and power pop, and in which Peter Criss discovers the cowbell. Despite its charms, this song never appeared on the Kiss setlist until well into the twenty-first century, by which time Criss had been and gone, and been and gone again.

'Watchin' You', also from Simmons, is a mediocre chugalong that never quite shrugs off its truly dreadful opening line, 'Limpin' as you do, and I'm watchin' you.' According to its composer, this ode to voyeurism was inspired by another Mountain song, 'Mississippi Queen', with lyrical inspiration from Alfred Hitchcock's *Rear Window* (1954). In truth, it is the cowbell-happy previous track that seems more obviously indebted to the Mountain song.

Stanley obviously took Simmons's lyrical clanger as a personal challenge and decided to come up with something better, by which we mean worse. He succeeds admirably, with Paul's 'I'm needing some loving, I'm hot like an oven' trumping Gene's limpin' line by some margin. 'Mainline' also triumphs over 'Watchin' You' because it rises above its risible lyric in a way the Simmons song does not, thanks to Stanley's ability to combine pop classicism with sashay and swagger. It is also elevated by Criss's soulful vocal, although he was only given the lead because he had threatened to quit the band otherwise.

'Comin' Home' is a Frehley-Stanley co-write, and is a sweet, simple song about a musician looking forward to getting back to his loved one at the end of a tour. It has the terrace-stomping bluster of Slade and features the kind of descending scale that Julian Cope later christened 'the glam descend'. Frehley obviously liked it, as he revisited it as 'What's on Your Mind?' on his 1978 solo.

'Strange Ways' is a Frehley track driven by the same kind of lumbering groove that would propel 'God of Thunder' a couple of years later. Criss handles the vocals, and the tub-thumper thought 'Strange Ways' would also benefit from an extended drum solo in the middle. When no one else agreed, he threatened to quit the band (again!). The solo was duly recorded and then promptly ditched once Criss had left the studio. Criss remained with the band, claiming in his autobiography that all he wanted was 'some input into the process', thus proving that cats could cry wolf too.

The *Hotter Than Hell* tour started a few days before the album's release and encompassed 51 shows in all. Along the way, they shared the stage with the likes of Black Oak Arkansas, Wishbone Ash, REO Speedwagon, and the James Gang. Notable dates include a couple in November with labelmates T. Rex, on what would be their final tour of the US; their one-off Casablanca album *Light of Love* would also be the last released in America in Bolan's lifetime. Kiss's New Year's Eve show at Evansville, Indiana, saw support from the Raspberries, whom Stanley has acknowledged as an influence.

This tour unexpectedly made the entertainment news in 2017 when Simmons attempted to trademark the 'devil horns' hand gesture, at least as far as live performances and appearances were concerned, claiming he had invented it during the '74 tour. However, the gesture was easily demonstrated to predate that year, being the American sign language symbol for 'I love you'. Even within music there were precedents, with several sources, including the *Music History Calendar* website, pointing out that John Lennon 'throws the horn' on the cover of The Beatles' 1966 'Yellow Submarine' single, and the two male members of the band Coven do likewise on the cover of their 1969 album *Witchcraft*. Simmons himself has said on several occasions that he lifted the gesture from how artist Steve Ditko drew Doctor Strange's hands when Marvel's superhero sorcerer cast a spell, which is identical to how Ditko drew Spider-Man shooting his web. To the surprise of surely no one, Simmons was unsuccessful.

1975: Dressed to Kill and Alive!

Dressed to Kill

Personnel:

Paul Stanley: rhythm guitar, vocals

Ace Frehley: lead guitar, vocals

Gene Simmons: bass, vocals

Peter Criss: drums, vocals

Recorded at Electric Lady Studios, New York City, February 1975

Produced by Neil Bogart and Kiss

Released: 19 March 1975

Running time: 30.07

Highest chart place: US: 32

Tracklisting: 1. 'Room Service' (Stanley) 2.59, 2. 'Two Timer' (Simmons) 2.47, 3. 'Ladies in Waiting' (Simmons) 2.35, 4. 'Getaway' (Frehley) 2.43, 5. 'Rock Bottom' (Frehley, Stanley) 3.54, 6. 'C'mon and Love Me' (Stanley) 2.57, 7. 'Anything for My Baby' (Stanley) 2.35, 8. 'She' (Simmons, Coronel) 4.08, 9. Love Her All I Can' (Stanley) 2.40, 10. 'Rock and Roll Al Nite' (Stanley, Simmons) 2.49

Alive!

Personnel:

Paul Stanley: rhythm guitar, vocals

Ace Frehley: lead guitar, vocals

Gene Simmons: bass, vocals

Peter Criss: drums, vocals

Recorded at the Cobo Arena, Detroit (16 May 1975), Cleveland Music Hall, Cleveland (21 June 1975), RKO Orpheum Theatre, Davenport (20 July, 1975), Wildwoods Convention Centre, Wildwoods (23 July 1975)

Mixed at Electric Lady Studio, New York City, August 1975

Produced by Eddie Kramer

Released: 10 September 1975

Running time: 78.17

Highest chart place: US: 9, UK: 49

Tracklisting: 1. 'Deuce' (Simmons) 3.32, 2. 'Stutter' (Stanley) 3.12, 3. 'Got to Choose' (Stanley) 3.35, 4. 'Hotter Than Hell' (Stanley) 3.11, 5. 'Firehouse' (Stanley) 3.42, 6. 'Nothin' to Lose' (Simmons) 3.23, 7. 'C'mon and Love Me' (Stanley) 2.52, 8. 'Parasite' (Frehley) 3.21, 9. 'She' (Simmons, Coronel) 6.42, 10. 'Watchin' You' (Simmons) 3.51, 11. '100,000 Years' (Stanley, Simmons) 12.12, 12. 'Black Diamond' (Stanley) 5.47, 13. 'Rock Bottom' (Frehley, Stanley) 3.08, 14. 'Cold Gin'

(Frehley) 5.21, 15. 'Rock and Roll All Nite' (Stanley, Simmons) 3.37, 16. 'Let Me Go, Rock and Roll' (Stanley, Simmons) 5.09

In an alternative universe, 1975 could have been the year that Kiss imploded. They may have been growing their audience at live shows, but their albums had sold poorly, sales on *Hotter Than Hell* having already bottomed out. Manager Bill Aucoin's American Express card was keeping the band on the road, but Kiss were as often as not the support act, sometimes even third on the bill, so box office receipts at best covered the cost of the show and wages for band and crew, and Aucoin was now a quarter of a million dollars in debt. Meanwhile, there were no royalties forthcoming from Casablanca, who were themselves looking into the financial abyss. The label had started as a subsidiary of Warner Brothers, but that relationship had ended when it became clear that Warner was prioritising its own acts at every stage, from the pressing plant to marketing. This meant that Casablanca was now truly an independent label and Neil Bogart could now run his company without interference from other stakeholders, but Warner had covered the cost of Casablanca's office rent, provided them with five Mercedes sedans, enabled them to sign and produce artists, and had paid for tour support for Kiss. They had also dealt with production, sales, and regional and national promotion for Casablanca's roster of artists, and all these functions and attendant costs now fell solely on Bogart and company.

Hotter Than Hell had failed to set the charts ablaze, and releases from the label's other acts, such as T. Rex, Parliament, Fanny, or the Hudson Brothers, had all underperformed. Bogart pinned his hopes on *Here's Johnny: Magic Moments from the Tonight Show*, a double album released in November '74 featuring audio clips from Johnny Carson's long-running talk show. However, television success didn't translate to the turntable, and *Here's Johnny* tanked.

A worried Bogart appeared at Kiss's show supporting Jo Jo Gunne on 1 February and ordered them back into the studio to make another album. Bogart himself would serve as producer, having dispensed with Richie Wise and Kenny Kerner's services, ostensibly because they had tried to lure Kiss to another label. The fact that it would keep costs down didn't hurt. Indeed, both Criss and Stanley have stated that Bogart's main contribution was to save money by preventing the band from doing too many takes, and that the actual production of the record fell to them.

Dressed to Kill was released the following month and featured another striking cover, this time a black and white shot of the band posing on a Manhattan corner in business suits and full makeup. Only Criss owned a suit, so the rest borrowed theirs from Aucoin, which explains why Simmons' is so ill-fitting. The photographer was Bob Gruen, whose most iconic photo is arguably that of John Lennon in dark shades and a white, sleeveless 'New York City' t-shirt. Gruen's then-wife Nadya supplied Gene with his clogs.

Stanley had heard that Canadian heavies Bachman-Turner Overdrive, then riding high with their *Not Fragile* album, used acoustic guitars to better define their sound, so one of Paul's first decisions in the producer's chair was to do the same. The first song to benefit from this was bouncy opener 'Room Service', a hymn to life on the road, and a more honest expression of that lifestyle than the cosy sentiments previously expressed in 'Comin' Home'. 'The joy of the vocal on 'Room Service' is real,' said the guitarist in *Face the Music*; 'I was celebrating the life we were living.'

Simmons' 'Two Timer' is up next, its content perfectly summed up in the title. It starts with grandiose rolling chords like those used in 'Goin' Blind', before Frehley and Stanley lay in with crosscut saw guitars. Once more, Gene jettisons his singing voice in favour of growling.

'Ladies in Waiting' is a title that Simmons had kicking around since the Wicked Lester days, but now, with a new album needed yesterday, necessity proved to be the mother of invention and he fleshed it out into a fully-fledged song. Actually, 'invention', 'fleshed out', and 'fully-fledged' is stretching it, as, like much of the material on *Dressed to Kill*, 'Ladies in Waiting' was short on verse and heavy on chorus, while lines such as 'So you've been to the market / And the meat looks good tonight' belies Simmons' later claim on an '80s edition of *Oprah* that there was mutual respect between group and groupie.

'Getaway' is Frehley's only solo contribution, a rollicking little rocker that presents the 'Should I stay or should I go' conundrum eight years before The Clash. With the English group the solution was a no-brainer, as the trouble would be doubled if they stay. With Frehley, there is no easy option, although he does inform the listener that he has 'no dough' and therefore might not be 'leavin' tomorrow by subway.' Anyway, Ace is still a mite shy, so Criss steps up to the microphone.

'Rock Bottom' is a cowrite, with Frehley responsible for the acoustic solo intro and Stanley the song proper. Frehley uses a Guild 12-string acoustic for his opening segment, which is not dissimilar to Ron Grainer's later, jauntier theme to the long-running British anthology television series *Tales of the Unexpected*, with Stanley providing the counterpart. Midway through, the song shifts gears and Stanley's punchy and altogether rockier half kicks in. It is an effective sonic one-two and one of the album's highlights.

'C'mon and Love Me' was the second single from the album, and early Kiss supporters *Cash Box* loved it: 'With ingenious lyrics, written from the sleazier side of being a rock star, Paul Stanley has written a blazing, high-energy rocker which illustrates why this group enjoys the fanatic, dedicated coterie it does. *You vill play it, you vill enjoy it*!' Perhaps they would have had they bought it, which nobody did. Amongst those 'ingenious lyrics' is the line 'I'm a Capricorn and she's a Cancer,' which acknowledges the Seventies fixation with star signs, a trend that later informed the lyrics of The Floaters' 1977 smash 'Float On' (US number two, UK number one). The guitar solo that launches 'C'mon and Love Me' was played by the songwriter, his first on a Kiss record, with Ace supplying the later solo.

Next up is 'Anything for My Baby', a song that also benefits from the BTO acoustic guitar embellishments. Stanley distanced himself from this song in later interviews, but it is a perfectly enjoyable glam stomper with a brash and bratty chorus, with a vocal that effectively combines vulnerability with sleaze. Some nice drum fills from Peter Criss too. It is probably the closest Kiss ever got to the New York Dolls, and it could have been a single contender.

'She' is a holdover from the Wicked Lester songbook and another instalment of Stephen Coronel's severance package. It is the longest song on the album, but quantity doesn't equal quality, and this is a bit of a dirge compared to the effervescence of the other tracks. Your reviewer prefers the Wicked Lester original, a borderline psych-rocker complete with flute and a superior vocal from both Simmons on lead and Stanley on backing. It is very much of a time and place, but that time and place sounds so much more interesting than what is presented here.

'Love Her All I Can' is another Wicked Lester leftover, but apart from a softer vocal approach in the original verse, there is not a lot to distinguish between the two. Again, Criss is very inventive in filling the space.

Neil Bogart asked Kiss to come up with a band anthem, like Sly and the Family Stone had done with 'Dance to the Music'. Stanley played a work-in-progress chorus to Simmons, and grafted it to a song fragment the latter had called 'Drive Me Wild'. The result was 'Rock and Roll All Nite', and it is safe to say they successfully met Bogart's criteria, although Simmons sees their song closer in tone to Slade's party anthems, right down to the deliberate misspelling of 'night'. 'Rock and Roll All Nite' was released as the first single from *Dressed to Kill*, with 'Getaway' on the flipside, and it cracked the charts. True, it stalled at 68, but it was a start, and it would revisit the listing later in the year. The album fared even better, climbing as high as 32 and spending 29 weeks on the *Billboard* 100.

During much of that chart residency, the band were on the road. Kiss also scored another nationwide television appearance when they recorded four songs for the *Mike Douglas Show* on 1 April. The band opted not to play 'Rock and Roll All Nite,' a baffling decision as it was due in stores the next day. Instead, *Dressed to Kill* was represented by 'She' and 'C'Mon and Love Me,' although the latter was never aired. 'Deuce' and 'Black Diamond' from their debut rounded out their performance, 'She' and 'Deuce' being broadcast on 11 July and 'Black Diamond' two months later. Meanwhile, their 16 May date at the Cobo Arena in Detroit was recorded for a live album, as were concerts at the Cleveland Music Hall (21 June), the RKO Orpheum Theatre, Davenport (20 July), and the Wildwoods Convention Centre, Wildwood (23 July).

The concept of a live album was nothing new, with the Beach Boys, Frank Sinatra, Grand Funk Railroad, the Allman Brothers Band, the Grateful Dead, and Black Oak Arkansas all having released one in the decade prior to 1975. But the live record was often dismissed as a way to buy breathing space between studio records, or worse, a contract fulfiller. Kiss, however, took their inspiration from across the pond, specifically the success of 1973's *Uriah Heep Live*, which peaked at 37 on the *Billboard* chart and was a worldwide success, and the previous year's *Slade Alive!*, which had given the Wolverhampton band their first UK and US chart entry (number two and, um, number 158 respectively). Kiss paid explicit homage to this last named by entitling their own concert document *Alive!* However, it was more the financial expediency of the live album rather than its storied history that provided the motivation; a new studio record would have cost more, and Kiss, Bill Aucoin, and Casablanca were running on empty.

The record hit stores on 10 September, and five days later, Aucoin decided to end the band's association with their record label, who had yet to pay Kiss any royalties. Bogart must have sensed that the tide was turning, and immediately issued a $2m cheque to keep them with Casablanca. His gamble paid off, as *Alive!* was a smash.

It has been claimed that the success of *Alive!* changed the music industry, with the concert document now viewed as a coveted live souvenir for the fan and a sure-fire winner for the record label. Certainly, Peter Frampton and Cheap Trick followed suit, scoring their greatest successes with *Frampton Comes Alive!* (1976) and *Cheap Trick at Budokan* (1978), and Bob Seger & the Silver Bullet Band, Led Zeppelin, Thin Lizzy, and Queen all released live albums in the wake of *Alive!* However, that is to overlook the success of *Uriah Heep Live* a little too conveniently, not to mention The Who's *Live at Leeds* (1970), Deep Purple's *Made in Japan* (1972) and *Yessongs* (1973), all of which went platinum in the United States. Better, then, to focus on what *Alive!* did achieve, which was to hit number 9 and to remain on the chart for an astonishing 110 weeks. It set the band on the road to superstardom and remains one of their biggest sellers. It also revived Casablanca's flagging fortunes, although the label was further bolstered by two other 1975 releases, Donna Summer's *Love To Love You Baby* and Parliament's *Mothership Connection*.

Certainly, the album was the best-sounding Kiss album to date, thanks in no small measure to Eddie Kramer being behind the console. The South African's many credits included producing Hendrix's *Electric Ladyland* and the posthumous *The Cry of Love*, and engineering *Led Zeppelin II*, *III*, and *Houses of the Holy*, not to mention Kiss's original five-track demo. Kramer had always been the band's first choice, but presumably, their diaries clashed. Although it was ultimately revealed that *Alive!* was the subject of some serious studio doctoring, with only Criss's drumming and Stanley's between-song banter reputedly surviving from the original tapes, Kramer was nonetheless able to capture the authentic sound of the band in a way the three tinnier studio albums had not. With the live set, there was no mistaking them for a glam or power pop band; Kramer cemented, if not outright established, their hard rock credentials.

Naturally, *Rolling Stone* hated it, their correspondent Alan Neister dismissing it as 'awful. Criminally repetitive, thuddingly monotonous'. However, perhaps in recognition of its role in launching a cultural phenomenon as much as its music, the same magazine placed *Alive!* at 159 in their 'greatest albums of all time' list of 2012, and number six in their 'greatest live albums' poll three years later.

Having a new album meant being back on the road to support it, and the 91-date trek around North America supporting *Alive!* opened in Chattanooga, Tennessee, on 10 September. For the first handful of dates, the opening act was Slade, whose influence on Kiss went beyond their similarly named live albums. Talking to *Metal Express Radio* in 2018, guitarist Dave Hill said, 'Gene Simmons has always said we were a big influence on them. He told me that before they started rehearsing, they'd listen to *Slade Alive!* to get them in the mood,' so it must have been even more inspirational to have the English rockers set the stage for them live.

One significant stop on the tour was at Cadillac, Michigan, on 9 October. The Cadillac High School football team, the Vikings, had a poor start to the season, so head coach Dave Brines and assistant coach Jim Neff hit upon the idea of playing Kiss records in the locker room before practices and games. Apart from being a fan, Neff liked that the band's name dovetailed with the old football credo of 'Keep It Simple, Stupid'. In true Hollywood style, the team won their remaining seven games. The story reached Bill Aucoin, who instantly saw its publicity possibilities, and Kiss were soon booked to play in the high school's gym as part of the city's homecoming parade.

Peter Criss tells it best in his autobiography *Makeup to Breakup*: 'We couldn't believe our eyes when we got to Cadillac that day. It was like living in KISSworld. Everybody was in our makeup – even the politicians and the people that worked behind the counters at the local McDonald's. We rode on a big float down a street that had been renamed KISS Boulevard. The mayor gave us the key to the city. We took pictures with the football team. And we carried along a sizeable number of press people who broke it into an international story'. The band's adventures in Cadillac would not be the only 1975 Kiss success story to have grassroots.

An aside: Forty years later, in 2015, coaches Brines and Neff were on hand to unveil a monument commemorating the event, a black granite monolith, eight feet by five, etched with the Kiss logo, photographs and signatures of the original band members, and details of the Vikings' 1974-1975 seasons. It is the only monument to the band in the world.

Five days after the Cadillac event, Kiss gained further momentum with the release of the live version of 'Rock and Roll All Nite'. By early 1976, it had climbed to number twelve in the singles chart, trouncing the studio version's meagre peak of 68.

Meanwhile, in November, on the banks of the Wabash, far away (actually, just across the state line from Michigan), a new element of the Kiss legend was being forged, and, as in Cadillac, the inspiration came not from the band or their management, but from two fans in Terre Haute, Indiana. Enter North Vigo High School students Bill Starkey and Jay Evans, respectively commander-in-chief and field marshal of the Kiss Army. The titles were self-bestowed, and the Kiss Army was basically them and some pals. Despite being too small and informal a group to even be recognised as a fan club, *USA Today* dubbed them 'rock and roll's original guerrilla marketing team'.

The Kiss Army is customarily accepted to have been founded on 21 November 1975, but this was a convenient date to give simply because it coincided with Kiss's first-ever concert in Terre Haute. The Army had in fact mobilised months before then, their mission to get Kiss records played on the city's WVTS. In their way stood an implacable enemy, program director Rich Dickerson, who dismissed the face-painted foursome as 'a mediocre Bachman-Turner Overdrive'. Starkey and Evans' strategy was to bombard the station with phone calls and letters demanding that their favourite band be played, with the occasional threat of blowing WVTS up thrown in to catch attention.

At face value, it reads like a classic case of 'the kids vs The Man', but the day was not really won due to the kids' communications blitzkrieg. Dickerson wasn't unyielding and was already bowing to the inevitable following the success of *Alive!*, the extensive coverage given the Cadillac event, the fact that a rival station was already giving the band rotation, and the upcoming Kiss gig. The show was at the Hulman Center, and the only act to sell out the arena since it opened two years previously was Elvis Presley. Dickerson decided to promote the concert by asking Starkey and Evans to write a series of over-the-top letters supporting Kiss, which he (Dickerson) would then read out on air before providing each with a mock shock-jock rebuttal. This created a buzz about the band, and the venue sold all its tickets.

Starkey met the band at the airport, joined them on air at WVTS, and was presented with an 'Honorary Kiss Member' plaque onstage (Jim Neff, the Vikings' assistant coach, had previously received this honour). But it was to be a pyrrhic victory for the Kiss Army's commander-in-chief, who entertained notions of running a nationwide Kiss Army. Despite initial encouragement from Bill Aucoin's Rock Steady Management, Aucoin soon handed control over to Boutwell Enterprises, and it was Ron Boutwell and Bill Aucoin that set Kiss on the road to being not just a band but a brand. In the Kiss autobiography *Behind the Mask*, Boutwell recalls the almost immediate success of the now official Kiss Army: 'We started doing two, three, four, five thousand dollars a day and the fan club was near a hundred thousand members. There was an article that came out in 1978 which said that Kiss had generated over $111 million in the retail sale of Kiss merchandise in 1978 alone.'

That was all in the future, though; in 1975, each member of Kiss was paid $75 per week.

Meanwhile, November gave way to December and the *Alive!* tour rumbled on, with support coming from, among others, old friends Rush, Styx (on the cusp of breaking big with their fifth album *Equinox*), and a Hoople-less Mott. On New Year's Eve, Kiss played the Nassau Coliseum in Uniondale, New York, where they were presented with their first gold record, for *Alive!* Their opening act was Blue Oyster Cult. Precisely two years earlier, the Cult had been the headliners, and Kiss fourth on the bill.

1976: Destroyer and Rock and Roll Over

Destroyer

Personnel:
Paul Stanley: rhythm guitar, vocals
Ace Frehley: lead guitar, vocals
Gene Simmons: bass, vocals
Peter Criss: drums, vocals
Additional personnel:
Dick Wagner: guitar solo on 'Sweet Pain', guitar on 'Flaming Youth', 'Great Expectations', and 'Beth'
Brooklyn Boys Choir: vocals on 'Great Expectations'
New York Philharmonic: orchestra on 'Beth'
David and Josh Ezrin: voices on 'God of Thunder'
Recorded at Record Plant Studios, New York City, September 1975, January and February 1976
Produced by Bob Ezrin
Released: 15 March 1976
Running time: 34.28
Highest chart places: US: 11, UK: 22
Tracklisting: 1. 'Detroit Rock City' (Stanley, Ezrin) 5.17, 2. 'King of the Night Time World' (Stanley, Fowley, Anthony, Ezrin) 3.19, 3. 'God of Thunder' (Stanley) 4.13, 4. 'Great Expectations' (Simmons, Ezrin) 4.24, 5. 'Flaming Youth' (Frehley, Stanley, Simmons, Ezrin) 2.59, 6. 'Sweet Pain' (Simmons) 3.20, 7. 'Shout It Out Loud' (Stanley, Simmons, Ezrin) 2.49, 8. 'Beth' (Criss, Penridge, Ezrin) 2.45, 9. 'Do You Love Me?' (Stanley, Fowley, Ezrin) 3.33, 10. 'Untitled track AKA Rock and Roll Party' (Simmons, Stanley, Ezrin) 1.25

Rock and Roll Over

Personnel:
Paul Stanley: rhythm guitar, vocals
Ace Frehley: lead guitar, vocals
Gene Simmons: bass, vocals
Peter Criss: drums, vocals
Recorded at Star Theatre, Nanuet, and Record Plant Studios, New York City, September-October 1976
Produced by Eddie Kramer
Released: 11 November 1976
Running time: 33.18

Highest chart place: US: 11

Tracklisting: 1. 'I Want You' (Stanley) 3.04, 2. 'Take Me' (Stanley, Delaney) 2.56, 3. 'Calling Dr. Love' (Simmons) 3.44, 4. 'Ladies Room' (Simmons) 3.27, 5. 'Baby Driver' (Criss, Penridge) 3.40, 6. 'Love 'Em and Leave 'Em' (Simmons) 3.47, 7. 'Mr. Speed' (Stanley, Delaney) 3.18, 8. 'See You in Your Dreams' (Simmons) 2.34, 9. 'Hard Luck Woman' (Stanley) 3.35, 10. 'Makin' Love' (Stanley, Delaney) 3.14

A reporter asked Paul Stanley, who didn't own a car and lived in rented accommodation, what it was like to be rich and famous. 'Well', he replied, 'I can tell you what it's like to be famous…'. That would soon change. 1976, the Bicentennial anniversary of the founding of the United States, was the year that Kiss got rich. Thanks to the newly established Kiss Army, they were about to become a marketing phenomenon, and in mid-March, they would release an album that would far exceed the success of *Alive!*.

Some preliminary work on this as-yet-untitled album had begun in September 1975, but the bulk of the recording took place in January 1976 during a break in the *Alive!* tour. At Bill Aucoin's suggestion, the producer was Bob Ezrin, then best known for his work on Alice Cooper's albums from *Love It To Death* on, and for being behind the console for *Berlin*, Lou Reed's adventurous, harrowing and potentially career-killing 1973 opus. All of Kiss were initially delighted to be paired with Ezrin but, for a couple of members of the band, the honeymoon would be short-lived.

Ezrin's approach to producing was different from anything Kiss had previously experienced. He called them 'campers' and wore a whistle around his neck, which he would blow whenever he would want them to start playing or to stop. To begin with, Stanley found his approach condescending: 'It was initially jarring to go into a studio with somebody who treated us like children'. He also wasn't above verbal aggression, famously once bawling Simmons out when the bassist stopped playing without Ezrin's permission.

However, both Stanley and Simmons came round to Ezrin's way of working, appreciating the opportunity to learn from him, as well as both his disciplined approach in the studio and the way he encouraged input from all members of the band and pushed their creativity. In this respect, his first edict was that they reject what Ezrin called their 'fuck me, suck me' lyrics (although going by the words to 'Sweet Pain' and 'Great Expectations', it is clear Simmons never read that memo). Another of Ezrin's aims, as he states in the liner notes of the *Destroyer* 45th anniversary boxset, was 'to expand the audience beyond fifteen-year-old boys and go after some girls too. We had to introduce a little pathos. We had to build a little more humanity into the group'.

Although both have nothing but praise for Ezrin now, Frehley and Criss hated working with him. Both guitarist and drummer would bandy about words and phrases like 'playing by feel' or 'spontaneity' and viewed their self-confessed inability to play the same thing twice as a badge of honour, which, as far as they were concerned, just made everything more 'rock and roll'. Ezrin's methodology was more measured and infinitely more painstaking; he would, for example, ask Frehley for multiple takes of a particular guitar solo, and then, rather than pick the best one, he would create his ideal version by stitching one together from the various takes at hand, like some musical Victor Frankenstein. The producer wanted considerably more intricate drum patterns to what Peter Criss had previously produced, and this, combined with multiple takes, took its physical toll on Criss, who would plunge his agonised hands into buckets of ice at the end of each session. In *Makeup to Breakup*, the drummer is unequivocal: 'Working with Ezrin was the hardest experience of my life'. In *No Regrets*, Frehley says that 'the recording process (of *Destroyer*) isn't something I recall with great affection. I was intimidated by Bob, especially when I couldn't come up with a guitar solo idea fast enough to suit his needs'. However, Ezrin could also prove to be a valuable mentor. In his memoir, Simmons remembers Ezrin stopping them in the middle of a rehearsal to give them a lesson in harmonic tuning and spending hours with Criss to teach him his drum parts.

23 January found the band back out on the road for the second leg of the *Alive!* tour, which started at Erie, Pennsylvania. Two days later they were back at Detroit's Cobo Arena for a three-night run, during which Stanley introduced the ritual of smashing a guitar at the end of the encore, a tradition that continued up to and including the band's *End of the Road* Tour. On 20 February, on a stopover in Los Angeles, Kiss dipped their hands in the cement outside Graumann's Chinese Theatre. It might appear odd to accord an honour usually reserved for the acting profession to a band only just tasting the fruits of success, but in truth, the ceremony had been devalued during the 1970s. Amongst a few obvious worthies such as George Burns and Jack Nicholson, other cement-dippers that decade included then mayor of Los Angeles and noted non-thespian Tom Bradley, plus a clutch of fictional characters including Herbie the Love Bug and a Star Wars trio consisting of Darth Vader, C-3PO, and R2-D2. In a shameless display of self-aggrandisement, Graumann's owner Ted Mann

cast his own handprints in stone the year after Kiss. After this short layoff, it was back on the road until 28 March, when the *Alive!* tour finally ended in Springfield, Massachusetts. By this time *Destroyer* had been on sale for two weeks.

Before moving on to the contents of the album, it is worth pausing to look at the package it was presented in, that now iconic purply-blue eye-popping cover by Ken Kelly that is arguably the most famous visual representation of the band. Ezrin may have wanted to sonically impart greater humanity upon Kiss, but album designer Dennis Woloch wanted to visually elevate them to gods and monsters, or even larger than larger-than-life rock and roll superheroes. Woloch's first choice of artist was Frank Frazetta, who had made his name painting covers for Warren Publishing magazines such as *Eerie*, *Creepy*, and *Vampirella*, as well as covers for Lancer's *Conan the Barbarian* paperback series issued between 1966 and 1977. Frazetta wanted $15,000 and sole ownership of the artwork, meaning that he would be paid anytime it was used in Kiss's ever-growing merchandising campaign. Woloch passed.

Now in need of an artist, Woloch headed to the nearest newsstand in search of inspiration. The cover of *Creepy* issue 72, featuring a solitary greenish-grey robot backlit by a raging fire, caught his eye. The colours popped out, and the way the artist had painted the main figure left it open to interpretation. The body language of the robot is such that one viewer could see him as lonely and dejected while another could see him as bristling with confidence. Those all-too-human eyes behind the faceplate could be equally pleading or defiant. Either way, Woloch had found his artist, and Ken Kelly was his name. By sheer coincidence, it turned out that Kelly was Frazetta's nephew by marriage.

This is the generally accepted version of how Ken Kelly got the *Destroyer* job, but Kelly added a new element to the tale when interviewed by *Print* magazine in 2018. As the artist understood it, it was Peter Criss and not Woloch's lunchtime newsstand trip that brought the artist to the attention of the band. Kelly had previously credited Simmons, but it was Criss who was a regular reader of Warren magazines, whereas Simmons was more of a Marvel fan.

Either way, Kelly was given a brief: the members of Kiss should be side-by-side to each other and leaping out toward the viewer. The poses of each member should reflect that person's onstage persona, and they should all be the same size. Behind the band, the artist was to paint the ruins of a city ablaze. Kelly did the job and got paid and then got a call a few days later telling him that Casablanca had rejected the cover. Someone had belatedly put two and two together and realised that, as it stood, the cover implied that Kiss had destroyed the city, and Casablanca didn't want their main cash cow to be seen as the bad guys. There was also the small matter of what they were wearing; all the photo references Kelly was given featured the *Alive!* outfits, but since being given the assignment Aucoin had commissioned new costumes for the band.

Woloch's solution was simple enough. Kelly was retained as the cover artist, and he was to keep the original poses of the band members, but now he was to paint them in their new stage gear, put them at the top of the mountain, and have the ruins, no longer ablaze, peaking out of the smoke in the distant background. It is a far superior version than the original, particularly in terms of the colour scheme – now blue and purple rather than brown – and especially regarding Kelly's vastly improved portrait of Frehley, but anyone viewing it will still conclude that the four guys in the foreground are responsible for all that destruction behind them.

Larry Legaspi hasn't entered our tale yet, so now is as good a time as any to introduce him. Legaspi was a fashion designer who specialised in giving his work a retro-futuristic science-fiction feel, and he first came to attention by designing costumes for Labelle following their transition from sweet soul singers to extraplanetary funkanauts. Bill Aucoin had decided to no longer rely on S&M shops, pet stores, and the needlework of relatives when it came to crafting Kiss's costumes and had contracted Legaspi based on his work for Labelle. The designer's first assignment had been the *Alive!* outfits, but with Kiss on the ascendant Legaspi was again tapped to create costumes that reflected the band's superstar status and which rejected their origins as part of the New York trash-glitter scene. The result was the *Destroyer* costumes, which, like Kelly's cover art, projected Woloch's vision of the band as sci-fi superheroes. These were Legaspi's last designs for Kiss, and he arguably never bettered them despite going on to work with Diana Ross, Grace Jones, Klaus Nomi, and Kiss's Casablanca labelmates Parliament – Funkadelic.

As if the costumes and the cover weren't enough, the music on *Destroyer* clearly denoted a major step-up in Kiss's evolution. The album opens with a newscast, read by Bob Ezrin, accompanied by odd background sounds, like a keyring full of keys being rattled in an echo chamber. 'In Detroit,' intones Ezrin solemnly, 'a Pontiac, Michigan youth was reported dead at the scene of a head-on collision on Grand Avenue this morning.' The listener is then informed that the young man was reportedly driving on the wrong side of the road when he collided with a delivery truck, and that the driver of the truck was uninjured. Ezrin fades out as he proceeds to read other news, but the drama just described is played out in sound effects, cutting from the car driven by the doomed youth (identifiable by his playing of, and singing along to, 'Rock and Roll All Nite') to the sound of the approaching delivery truck and back again, before the guitars that open 'Detroit Rock City' come into play, increasing in volume until joined by the rhythm section. Ezrin's influence is immediately felt; even leaving aside the sound effects, the production is worlds away from the weediness of *Kiss*, *Hotter Than Hell*, and *Dressed to Kill*. Kiss have never sounded so good. There is a complexity to the drums and bass playing far beyond anything on the first three albums, with Simmons and Criss sounding crisp, powerful, and very much to the fore. There is almost a sense of role-reversal, with Stanley and Frehley's guitars playing timekeepers to the rhythm section. When Stanley starts singing, it is like his pipes have received an upgrade to match his rhinestone-studded outfit, as for the first time, he sounds not just like a singer with the band and more like the frontman for a stadium-filling behemoth.

The song follows the last few hours in the protagonist's life, with the clock counting down from 9 pm to midnight and his inevitable encounter with the delivery truck. When Stanley presented the song to Ezrin, the title – a play on Detroit's usual nickname of 'Motor City' – was in place, as was the 'get up, get down' section, but it was lyrically undernourished and essentially a party-happy number in the vein of 'Rock and Roll All Nite'. When discussing the song with Ezrin, Stanley recalled hearing of a Kiss fan that had been killed *enroute* to a concert, and the producer suggested that become the basis for the lyric. Despite the mention of drinking (and possibly drugging) before driving, Ezrin didn't want the words to 'glorify getting fucked up – I have kids and I have always been very much aware of my responsibility as someone that makes records, and I've never wanted to glorify that'. This presumably was a sentiment that Stanley and Simmons would agree with. For the record, the producer wasn't keen on the album's title for much the same reason, thinking the word 'destroyer' had too negative a connotation.

Returning briefly to the unfortunate Kiss fan that inspired the lyric, it appears he (and in 1974 or 1975, it would almost certainly have been a 'he') is just a figment of the greater Kiss mythology. James Campion, who wrote the authoritative and indispensable *Shout It Out Loud: The Story of Kiss's Destroyer and the Making of an American Icon*, conducted exhaustive research to discover this fan's identity by matching police and newspaper reports of car crash fatalities to Kiss concert appearances in Charlotte – where Stanley has repeatedly said he believes the crash to have occurred – and other North Carolina cities, and came up with nothing. This is not to say that Stanley is guilty of fabrication, as he may simply have got the location wrong, and Campion interviewed Kiss crew members from that period who also recalled hearing of a young fan's death in an automobile accident. However, they only remember it being something that circulated amongst team Kiss; no one can remember reading about it in a newspaper or hearing it on the radio, *a la* Ezrin's introduction to the song.

Returning to the song, one of the highlights of 'Detroit Rock City' is Stanley and Frehley's flamenco-flecked guitar duet, but neither man wrote it. As Ace recounts in *No Regrets*: 'As a guitar player, this is hard for me to admit, but the solo on 'Detroit Rock City' is one of the single best moments in any Kiss song. And I had nothing to do with creating it. I wish I had thought of it, but I didn't. It was all Bob's'. According to Stanley's memoir *Face the Music*, Ezrin wrote the solo and then taught it to him and Frehley. The producer is also credited with coming up with the bass part.

Ezrin ends 'Detroit Rock City' with sound effects signifying the fatal car crash, a clever sonic bookend to the newscast that opened the song. Above the sounds of smashing glass and grinding metal is a sustained guitar note, like a banshee at the site of a death foretold, and this guitar effect carries the listener into the next track, 'King of the Night Time World'. It occupies the centre channel and is soon joined by a guitar on the left, followed by one on the right. Criss fills the space behind the guitars with a tremendous drum fill, all of which creates a joyous cacophony that carries the listener beyond the tragedy of the first track. There is no bass, and Simmons remains out of the picture until the chorus. When Stanley starts the opening verse, his vocals are double-tracked, giving the song greater density. It equals the album opener in terms of drama and grandiosity and sounds like an instant Kiss classic in the making, but 'King of the Night Time World' is a cover version.

It was originally recorded by the Hollywood Stars for their unreleased 1974 album *Shine Like a Radio* and was written by Stars guitarist Mark Anthony and L.A. impresario Kim Fowley. When the Stars split up, Fowley offered the song to Kiss via Bob Ezrin. Ezrin thought it would be a suitable vehicle for Paul Stanley, who agreed, believing the song to be in tune with 'the attitude of the band' and 'in keeping with my personality'.

Some changes were made to the arrangement – the introduction to the song described above is very different from the Stars' original – and to the words. Stanley takes the slightly clunky opening line, 'It's so bad, just goin' to school / Far from me and the pleasures that we've done' and sprinkles in some added sleaze to get, 'So far from me and the dirty things that we've done'. Elsewhere, he emphasises the song's nighttime setting by replacing the fey 'Far from the music and the gorgeous clothes' with 'Far from the music and the neon glow'. There are other changes to the words and music, but the net effect is that Kiss took a very good power pop song and gave it a coliseum-sized upgrade, polishing it until it dazzled.

Whether any of these musical or lyrical alterations warrant Stanley and Ezrin a co-writing credit is a moot point; Anthony and Fowley could let 'King of the Night Time World' gather dust on a studio shelf, or they could sell some of their shares in the song and make money from it. Unsurprisingly, they did the latter. Kiss would cut a similar deal with Russ Ballard fifteen years later when they covered 'God Gave Rock and Roll to You'.

Speaking of gods... One of the songs Paul Stanley brought to the *Destroyer* sessions was called 'God of Thunder and Rock and Roll', a ditty he fancied would become his signature song. Ezrin gave the demo a spin and said, 'Oh, that's great. That's for Gene'. 'I was just devastated', Stanley told *Rock Candy* in 2022. 'The idea of a song so quickly being passed off from me to someone else… It was difficult, and it remained a sore point, even when I heard it finished'. However, one of the rules Kiss had set themselves was that the producer's word was final, so Simmons got to sing the snappily renamed 'God of Thunder', and it has since become *his* signature song.

'God of Thunder' opens with a child's voice high on excitement, part cherubic, part infernal, and creepy as hell. It commands the band to start singing, and they oblige with a thudding menacing riff that recalls some vaudevillian Native American war dance more than it does a Northern Germanic hammer-wielding deity. Simmons opts to sing in his most diabolical growl, and this, plus Ezrin's decision to slow the pace, confirms that the producer called it right. Simmons prowls his hellish wasteland with relish, with Ezrin adding howls of distorted guitar and reversed drums to further invoke this nightmarish realm. Criss's ominous drumming completes the picture, appropriately conjuring forth rolling thunder, and the original demonic cherub is joined by a second, ghost children from another dimension chattering back and forth, both a part of the song and quite apart from it. When the guitar solo kicks in, it is, to paraphrase W. B. Yeats, like some rough beast awakening and slouching towards Bethlehem to be reborn. 'God of Thunder' is a superb piece of aural theatre, indicative of both the band's maturation and Ezrin's skill as producer.

To his credit, Stanley altered the lyrics to best reflect Simmons' Demon persona. Thus, a line like 'I was raised by the women / I live for pleasure and fun', which was entirely suited to Stanley's Starchild / Lover persona, was changed to the more sinister 'I was raised by the demons / Trained to reign as the one / God of Thunder'. Despite his initial disappointment, Stanley came round to Ezrin's way of thinking: 'In hindsight, it couldn't have been a better move', he said. 'It's such a character-defining song for Gene, and he did it so great. Sometimes you're lucky to be wrong'.

Those wonderfully evocative background voices were provided by Ezrin's kids, David and Josh, then aged ten and eight respectively, playing with a cheap walkie-talkie set. They previously appeared on Lou Reed's *Berlin* album, also produced by Ezrin, as the children crying for their mother on the song 'The Kids'. Despite his clear and substantial contributions to 'God of Thunder', this is one of only two songs on *Destroyer* that does not include an Ezrin co-writer credit.

Side one closes with what is surely the most outlier song in the Kiss canon to date, 'Great Expectations'. This was based on an earlier Simmons song, the cheerfully titled 'You've Got Nothing to Live For', but it became something infinitely more substantial once Ezrin got his hands on it. Lyrically it veers close to the 'you wanna have sex with me' nonsense that Ezrin had asked the songwriters in the group to avoid, but even in its original demo, it was surprisingly more tender than one might expect a song about a groupie to be. And yes, you read that right; 'Simmons' and 'tender', all in the same paragraph.

'Great Expectations' is credited to Simmons and Ezrin, but a certain Ludwig van Beethoven should also get a shout-out as Ezrin skilfully grafts a snippet of the German composer's Piano Sonata No. 8 in C Minor (aka *Sonata Pathétique*) onto the introduction of the song. With its acoustic guitars, piano, glockenspiel, and orchestra, and a lovely nine-note guitar solo that again channels Beethoven's sonata, this is the band's only foray into baroque and roll, and it is an absolute gem. The moment Simmons unexpectedly hands the microphone over to the Brooklyn Boys Choir borders on heart-stopping.

The original words had Paul singing his song, Ace playing his guitar, and Peter beating his drums, and whoever decided to jettison these painfully crass lyrics should be lauded. The replacement lyrics, with just Simmons singing the song, playing his guitar, and beating his drum are still undeniably crass, but placed atop the song's sumptuous soundscape, they are charmingly crass without the suggestion of gangbanging.

The complex arrangement of 'Great Expectations' means that the song has only ever been played once live, at a 2003 concert when Kiss were accompanied by the Melbourne Symphony Orchestra, with the Australian Children's Choir subbing for their Brooklyn predecessors.

Side two opens strongly with 'Flaming Youth', which took its name from an early Kiss support band and was pieced together Frankenstein-style with fragments from Stanley and Frehley stitched onto the remains of an earlier Simmons song called 'Mad Dog'. It is a bratty and unabashed glam rocker that could be seen as a less suicidal successor to 'All the Young Dudes' (providing you chose to view 'Dudes' as a youth anthem and not the continuation of the apocalyptic 'Five Years' that Bowie said it was). Ezrin's contribution was to prominently feature a calliope which didn't go down well with the band but which nonetheless gives the song a distinct identity.

'Flaming Youth' was Frehley's only writing credit on *Destroyer* and one he shared with three other people, a far cry from his solo credits from the first three studio albums. This lack of creativity on the guitarist's part was a sign that he was succumbing to the drugs and booze, and his disconnection from the recording process is further evinced by Ezrin's hiring of Lou Reed / Alice Cooper sideman Dick Wagner to provide some extra guitar licks on this track.

'Sweet Pain' is a further indication that Simmons hadn't received the 'no more songs about sex' message, but Ezrin let it make the cut after sweetening the track with some shamefully uncredited female backing vocals. What didn't make the cut was Frehley's guitar solo. 'I had done a solo on 'Sweet Pain' and it was okay', he told Ken Sharp for *Behind the Mask*. 'I said, 'Maybe I'll come in tomorrow and take another shot at it''. That lackadaisical 'maybe' would hardly have impressed Ezrin, Stanley, and Simmons, so it's perhaps no surprise that Ezrin dialled Wagner to report for duty, this time to lay down the guitar solo. Several years later, when talking about the *Destroyer* sessions in his autobiography *No Regrets*,

Frehley was unrepentant about his behaviour. He was 'living the life of a rock star', he says, seemingly oblivious to the fact that making records is probably the most fundamental part of that life.

In their respective memoirs, both Criss and Stanley remember Frehley ducking out of *Destroyer* sessions so that he could play cards with friends. 'I couldn't get my head around that at all', wrote Stanley. 'Leaving the job to get loaded and play cards, even if it meant having another guitar player handle his part? Making music was my dream, and skipping out on the process was something I couldn't fathom'. The version of 'Sweet Pain' containing Frehley's solo saw the light of day with the release of *Destroyer: Resurrected* in 2012.

'Shout It Out Loud' is an anthemic youthfest hewn from the same rockface as 'Flaming Youth' and 'Rock and Roll All Nite'. It was released as the first single from *Destroyer*, presumably chosen to capitalise on the success of the live version of the latter track. While not as successful as its predecessor, 'Shout It Out Loud' charted at a respectable number 31 in the US. More significantly, it gave Kiss their first number one by topping the Canadian chart, and served as their debut placing in the New Zealand, German, and Swedish listings. The title is likely inspired by the Hollies song 'I Wanna Shout', which was covered by Wicked Lester as '(We Wanna) Shout It Out Loud'.

The next track is the band's first ever ballad, 'Beth', which was written by Peter Criss and Stan Penridge during their days in Chelsea, when it was originally called 'Beck'. According to Penridge, talking to *KissFAQ*, Chelsea's guitarist Mike Brand was constantly getting interrupted during band practice by his wife, Becky, asking him when he was coming home. Most of the lyrics are based on Brand's responses to Becky, which Penridge wrote down in his notebook for future use.

Bob Ezrin has been surefooted as producer so far, but with 'Beth' he missteps. He unceremoniously jettisons all of Kiss bar Criss, places himself behind the piano and assigns acoustic guitar duties to Dick Wagner, and then slathers the song in strings and syrup. It is simply awful, and it would be too easy to blame the songwriters, but the Chelsea demo found online has a folksy arrangement, a raw lead vocal, truly excellent harmonies, and an interesting use of tom-toms throughout, and is thoroughly enjoyable. Ezrin should have been less concerned about tinkering with it so that he could get a co-writing credit, and more concerned about ensuring 'Beth' was arranged to involve all the band, and the template to do that was right there in the original demo.

Ezrin's sickly-sweet presentation gained a fan in Casablanca promoter Scott Shannon, who, when asked by label president Neil Bogart what he thought should be the third single from *Destroyer*, unhesitatingly opted for 'Beth'. Or, depending on whose account you read, Shannon got the thumbs up for 'Beth' from Rosalie Trombley, the music director for Canadian radio station CKLW, whose ear for a hit had already helped the careers of Alice Cooper, Bob Seger and Elton John. Either way, Bogart baulked at the suggestion, as Beth was also the name of his ex-wife and the lyrics too closely resembled things said during divorce proceedings. Bogart decided on 'Detroit Rock City' as the next single and buried 'Beth' on the B-side.

Now a phenomenon that became part of Kiss lore occurred, as DJs across America rejected 'Detroit Rock City' and spun 'Beth' instead. Listeners started inundating radio stations with requests for the ballad, and Casablanca swiftly reissued the single, but with 'Beth' now promoted to the A-side. If this turn of events proved painful for Bogart, he could at least take solace that 'Beth' went to number seven, went gold, reignited the sales of *Destroyer*, and won a 1977 People's Choice Award. Just as *Destroyer* had bestowed Simmons with his signature song in 'God of Thunder', it now did the same with Peter Criss and 'Beth'.

'Beth' seems to be a surprisingly polarising song for Kiss members to this day. In *No Regrets*, Frehley says he thought 'Beth' was a good song that 'deserved to be a hit'. 'I have nothing bad to say about 'Beth'', he continued. 'It was a solid ballad, and a perfect complement to the hard-driving rock that made up 95 per cent of our live show'. Significantly, Frehley concludes that he was happy for Criss.

Simmons' reaction to 'Beth' is harder to gauge. Frehley reports that 'Gene actually thought it was interesting – enough of a departure that it might help serve *Destroyer*'s mission, which was to move the band in a slightly different direction'. In their biography of Bogart, *Going Platinum*, Brett Ermilio and Josh Levine state that Simmons, along with Stanley, 'wasn't impressed with the song', and 'believed it to be too 'soft sounding' for the album'. In his own memoir, Simmons calls 'Beth' a 'nice little melody' and states he suggested the name change so that no one would think the song was about Jeff Beck, but his focus was less on the song and more on the production: 'The only way we validated the idea that there were strings on it was because of 'Yesterday' by the Beatles. If it was cool for the Beatles, then we could do it'.

Stanley, whose *Face the Music* memoir is generally regarded as being the most even-handed of the four band autobiographies, lets himself down when discussing 'Beth', which he takes as an invitation to belittle Criss. He starts somewhat pointlessly with the original title: 'What's a Beck?!', he rhetorically asked *Classic Rock* in 2005. 'It just wasn't a name that people could relate to'. Stanley would christen a girl in one of the songs on the next album Rags, so it is safe to apply the pot-kettle-black equation here. Also, if that's your line of criticism, an obvious retort could be, 'What's a Starchild?' Stanley would get particularly vicious when contesting Criss's songwriting credit. Here he is talking to *Rolling Stone* in 2014: 'Peter had nothing to do with it. It was a lifeline that Peter hung on to validate himself, but it wasn't based on reality'. And in *Face the Music*: 'Bob (Ezrin) wrote the lion's share of 'Beth'...'. Again, a quick listen to the Chelsea demo will soon disabuse that notion, and it is a surprising stance for Stanley to take, considering he bought himself a credit on the Hollywood Stars' 'King of the Night Time World' *on the very same album*.

Let's give Criss's former wife Lydia the last word in the 'Who wrote Beth' non-controversy. Talking to the *Legendary Rock Interviews* website in 2013, she said that 'Stan Penridge was the main one behind that. Peter might have written some of the words, but Stan Penridge wrote the music... As far as the lyrics, I actually wrote a line in that song and never got credit. I wrote, 'You say you feel so empty' because I did feel that way.'

From this, we can conclude that Penridge wrote the melody and primarily wrote the lyrics with some assistance from Criss (and possibly Lydia), and Ezrin brought the 'If George Martin was a Disney character' arrangement to the table. What is unequivocal is the impact 'Beth' had. Casablanca vice-president Larry Harris had this to say in *And Party Every Day*, his history of the label: 'I cannot overemphasise how important that song was to Kiss's eventual achievement of superstardom. And it shoved Casablanca several rungs up the prestige ladder in the process. In fact, without 'Beth', it's entirely possible that Kiss would soon have found themselves in the 'Where are they now' category'.

From the insecurity of the antagonist to the insecurity of the narrator. It is Criss's propulsive drums, echoed to the max, that introduce the last song on *Destroyer*, 'Do You Love Me', and serves as Stanley's sole accompaniment during the first verse. Addressing an unnamed woman, an uncertain Stanley notes she likes going to the shows and the limousines and that she even likes his seven-inch leather heels. In later verses, he lists all the other things she likes, like the credit cards, the private planes, the hotels, the fancy clothes, and 'all the money, honey, that I make'. However, there is a 'but' coming up, and it is surely the biggest 'but' in rock history. 'BUT!', screeches Stanley, 'Do you love me?'

Interviewed for James Campion's *Shout It Out Loud*, Bob Ezrin recalled: 'In my head, onstage, I could almost see Paul getting down on his knees and shouting 'Do you love me?' I just visualised all the girls running to the front and throwing their bras at him, screaming, 'I love you, Paul!' I just thought that was the thing that was going to open up the floodgates for us, that was going to make them human enough to become romantic figures to the women in the audience'. Whether 'Do You Love Me?' did transform Kiss into 'romantic figures' is debatable, but it allowed Stanley to project a degree of vulnerability that would have been unthinkable on previous albums, and it provided *Destroyer* with a satisfying album closer.

Except, it didn't quite close the album. *Destroyer* clocked in at just over thirty minutes, so Ezrin expanded it by creating the introduction to 'Detroit Rock City' and by also allowing engineer Jay Messina to add a coda, a hidden track that has come to be known as 'Rock and Roll Party'. This basically consists of ambient loops and sound effects, the most obvious of which are crowd sounds and a snippet of Stanley's onstage banter, 'I tell you, people, we're just gonna have ourselves a rock and roll paw-ty', while a ghostly version of the Brooklyn Boys Choir reprises the chorus of 'Great Expectations'. Apart from its primary function of clocking up the minutes, 'Rock and Roll Party' provides a surprisingly atmospheric denouement to *Destroyer*.

The album was released on 16 March to less than favourable reviews. Robert Christgau starts promisingly in *The Village Voice*, stating that 'these guys have always rocked better than adults were willing to enjoy' before concluding that *Destroyer* was 'their least interesting record', and slating Ezrin's production for adding only 'bombast and melodrama'. *Melody Maker*'s Harry Docherty, despite thinking 'Great Expectations' and 'Beth' showed 'intelligent use of orchestra and choir', concluded that the band's future would be brief, based on 'the level of staidness displayed on *Destroyer*'. John Milward of *Rolling Stone* was merciless: 'The songs, save for two bloated ballads, are relentless riff rockers rooted in patently pedestrian drumming. The vocals are undistinguished and emotionally empty, the lyrics trite'.

Even the friendlies were anti-*Destroyer*, with Rick Johnson of *Creem* accusing Ezrin of robbing the band of their 'rusty coat-hanger appeal' before concluding that, 'This ain't the scuzzy Kiss we all came to love (and hate) so well'. Robert Duncan of *Circus* was even more damning: 'The new Kiss album stinks'.

A backlash also came from the fans. Having decried the earlier albums as sounding tinny or weedy, they now denounced *Destroyer* as too arranged, too polished. Choirs, orchestras, and ballads apparently had no place on a Kiss album. 'One Kiss fan told me that if he ever met me, he would punch me in the nose on behalf of Kiss fans everywhere', Ezrin told *Ultimate Classic Rock* years later. 'The core of the Kiss Army at the time was offended and angry, and particularly angry with me for having taken Kiss in a new direction.'

In terms of sales, the album initially performed well. It cracked the top tens of Canada, Australia, and Sweden, and even reached 22 in the United Kingdom, a country that was largely impervious to Kiss's charms throughout the '70s. On home territory, it became a gold-selling album by late April and reached its number 11 peak the following month. Then it went into freefall. By the time 'Beth' was released in August, *Destroyer* was languishing at 192 and would briefly drop out of the 200 altogether. There is the perception that the success of 'Beth' sent its parent album soaring back into the top thirty, but that is far from the case. *Destroyer* re-entered the chart at 133 on 2 October and lurked below the top one hundred for a further eleven weeks, only breaching it at the end of the year. It did eventually reach a new peak of 37 in February 1977 and remained on the chart for a further eight weeks.

It is this second, protracted run on the charts – a run of continuing steady sales – that is usually credited to the success of 'Beth'. Says Simmons in *Kiss and Make-Up*: 'Our lifestyle changed drastically after *Destroyer*, especially after the boost from 'Beth'. I bought houses for both my parents, even though I hadn't seen my father since he left me as a child in Israel'. Stanley was similarly able to treat his parents in the wake of *Destroyer*. 'I bought my parents a Chrysler. It was the first time they had ever owned a new car. I also bought them a house not long after, when my dad lost his job – and his pension. Instead of possibly being on welfare and food stamps, they were in a new house, with a new car'. Touchingly, Criss bought a marble headstone for his grandmother's grave site, as his parents hadn't been able to afford one when she died.

The first leg of the *Destroyer* tour, also known as the 'Spirit of '76 Tour', began on 11 April in Fort Wayne, Indiana and ran through to 28 April, with a very important date on the first day of May. Chris Lendt, then part of Kiss's financial team, describes the occasion in his book *Kiss and Sell: The Making of a Supergroup*:

> His (Frehley's) wedding to Jeanette Trerotola, an Italian girl from suburban New York, was a huge affair at New York's Americana Hotel that attempted to link two sharply different worlds. Ace and his pals, many with long scruffy hair and bizarre clothes, symbolised the rock world. Jeanette came from a large family. At the wedding, many relatives showed up, including her grandfather, Joe Trerotola, one of the highest-ranking officials in the Teamsters who was known as Joe T. Her father, Vinnie, was also a Teamsters official. At times the two camps appeared to face off against each other, with each group congregating separately on opposite sides of the large hotel ballroom.

Criss, Simmons and Stanley were all in attendance, and at one point, they borrowed the wedding band's instruments to play impromptu versions of 'Strutter', 'Nothin' to Lose' and 'Rock and Roll All Nite'. Footage of the latter can be found online and ably demonstrates that Kiss were far from the hottest wedding band in the land. They left the stage after Vinnie Trerotola asked them to stop detracting from his daughter's wedding festivities.

There was no time for a honeymoon as the following week, Kiss began their first European tour. They disembarked from the plane at London's Heathrow Airport in full make-up – they were still using the *Alive!* outfits at this time – to meet the press and were then whisked off to Buckingham Palace and Westminster Bridge for some publicity shots. 'I was in awe', Simmons recounted in *Kiss and Make-Up*, 'because it was England, the home of the Beatles'. Stanley was similarly starstruck in *Face the Music*: 'To me, England represented the musical holy land'.

Reality soon trampled on such romanticism. Stanley: 'The food was horrible and the transportation archaic. Merchants took perverse pride in the fact that you couldn't get dry cleaning back for a week. There was no air conditioning, and, if you pleaded, they might begrudgingly put a lone ice cube in a drink for you'. Worst of all, they were still relatively unknowns in Europe, playing, as Criss put it, 'filthy, half-filled shit-holes'. This wasn't entirely true; Kiss sold out all four concerts in England, but the capacity of the venues was minuscule compared to what they had become accustomed to. It was a rude awakening for a band already fancying themselves as superstars.

One indicator of their lowly status in Europe was their Paris Olympia show on 22 May, which started at 3 pm to accommodate Jerry Lewis's evening booking. In his memoir, Criss generously suggests that Kiss opened for the American comedian, but in fact, they and their stage set had to be out of the venue by 6 pm to allow Lewis's people time to set up. The situation was better in Sweden, where *Destroyer* would peak at number four. In her book *Sealed with a Kiss*, Lydia Criss describes the scene at the Gothenburg gig: 'Through the entire show, no one clapped or showed any emotion, and then, at the very end of the concert, the fans went wild, breaking chairs and throwing them onstage at the band. The promoter told us this was the way the fans let you know they liked you'. Two days later, they were playing the Tivoli Gardens in Stockholm to a capacity crowd of 15,600, which was more in keeping with their American numbers. Kiss also played shows in Germany, Holland, Denmark, and Switzerland, but the nadir of the tour was the last European date in Harelbeke, Belgium, where they played to an audience of less than 500.

Returning Stateside, the foursome had a fortnight off before the second leg of their North American jaunt kicked off, although on 24 June, they participated in a photoshoot that resulted in one of their most iconic images, Kiss, now in their Destroyer outfits, on top of the Empire State Building.

Talking to Sweden's *Poster-Story* website, photographer Barry Levine cites the Empire State Building photo shoot as his favourite. 'We just thought that we were going to shoot it on that level that everyone attends. Then the managers of the building said, 'you know that there is one more level above that is a private level'. We went up there and it had a very little ledge, a thin ledge, but if you fall over, you fall like maybe five feet to another ledge, a wide ledge. But because of the perspective, I was shooting, it didn't look like that. It looked like we were right on the very edge. I had two of their bodyguards hoist me up on their shoulders so I could shoot from that perspective. We had very little room to shoot. That was my favourite photo of all time.' Despite this hidden ledge, Stanley was alarmingly frank on *kissonline.com*: 'We were all scared shitless. You could see one arm and one hand of each guy, and the other hand was holding on for dear life'.

Levine also shot the 'Spirit of '76' photo, based loosely on Archibald Willard's famous painting of the same name. In the *Destroyer 45th Anniversary Super Deluxe* boxset, Simmons recalls 'Ace holding onto me for dear life, because he was drunk and could barely stand up and he couldn't stop laughing about nothing in particular'. This image was sold as a poster on the *Destroyer* tour and, along with the tour book, is one of the first items of official Kiss merchandise.

The *Destroyer* tour ended on 12 September at Springfield, Massachusetts, with support from five-piece power poppers Artful Dodger, who had also supported at thc opening gig back in April. They had played on some of the shows in-between, but the main support act for the bulk of the tour was Bob Seger and the Silver Bullet Band, who, along with Ted Nugent and Montrose (subbing for late pull-outs Uriah Heep), were on the bill at Kiss's biggest show to date. This was on 20 August, when their concert at Anaheim Stadium drew just under 43,000 people. According to the excellent *Kiss Concert History Online* site, merchandise sales alone amounted to $35,850, which accounted for 16% of total merchandising sales for the whole tour. These figures presumably laid to rest the ghost of Belgium.

Hindsight is a wonderful thing. Here's Peter Criss's assessment of *Destroyer*, taken from his autobiography: '*Destroyer* was our *White Album*'. Here's Ace Frehley, interviewed by Ken Sharp for the 45th-anniversary boxset: 'I think the reason *Destroyer* holds up so many decades later has to do with working with Bob, his writing ability and ability to take us, musically, to another level'. And finally, from the same source, here's Stanley: 'Whenever I'm in the studio, I find myself saying 'What would Bob do?' and to me, that's about the biggest compliment that I can give somebody'. One would think, with all these kudos, Ezrin would be the obvious choice to produce the band's follow-up to *Destroyer*, but Kiss was having none of it.

Simmons: 'Ace and Peter were pressing us to get back to basics, to being a four-piece rock and roll band without arrangements, ballads, or someone else telling us how to play'. Stanley: 'Maybe we didn't want to have a nanny this time around – someone telling us how to do everything and blowing a whistle in our faces. We figured we'd done our apprenticeship. And Peter and Ace certainly had no desire to work with Bob again'. Interviewed for the 45th-anniversary boxset, Simmons elucidates: 'Paul was concerned that *Destroyer* was too symphonic and too arranged and didn't have the original sound of the band. So, it was Paul who said, 'Let's go back with Eddie Kramer, the guy who did our big seller *Alive!*, and do a more rock and roll record'.'

So, Ezrin was out and Kramer was in, although it wasn't quite that straightforward. According to Stanley, their first choice was Jack Douglas,

Left: Kiss in London at the start of their first international tour in May 1976. They would rehearse at Shepperton Studios, where filming was also taking place on the first *Star Wars* movie.

Right: At the end of the decade, Kiss scrapped their trademark black and silver outfits for costumes that put the nasty in *Dynasty*.

Left: The Kiss Army logo, proudly emblazoned on many a '70s denim jacket, was designed by long-time Kiss art director Dennis Woloch and Vincent DiGerlando. *(Kiss Catalog Ltd)*

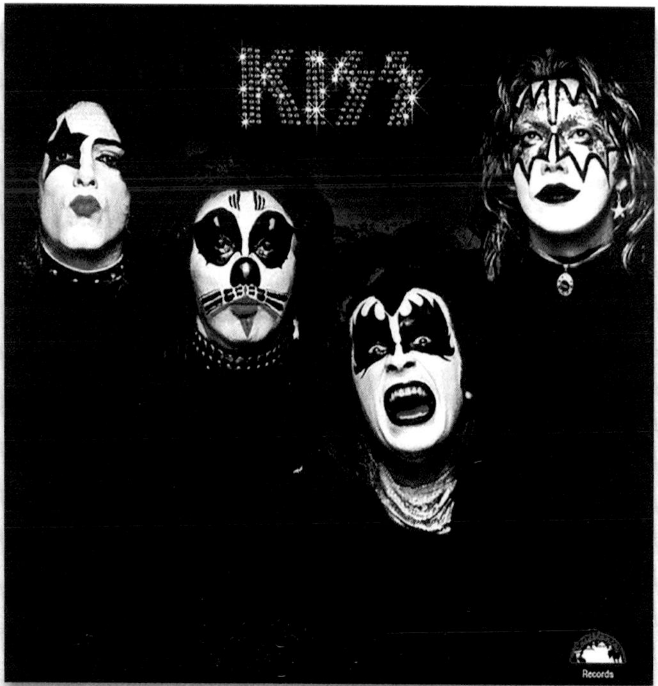

Left: Despite substandard production, *Kiss* was a strong debut, with several of its songs remaining setlist staples throughout the band's career. *(Universal Music Enterprises / Mercury Records / Kiss Catalog Ltd)*

Right: Like its predecessor, *Hotter Than Hell* got the cold shoulder from the record-buying public. Kiss's success as a live act wasn't reflected by their album sales. *(Universal Music Enterprises / Mercury Records / Kiss Catalog Ltd)*

Right: *Dressed to Kill* they may be, but at this stage in their career, Gene, Paul, and Ace couldn't afford their own suits so had to borrow Bill Aucoin's. *(Universal Music Enterprises / Mercury Records / Kiss Catalog Ltd)*

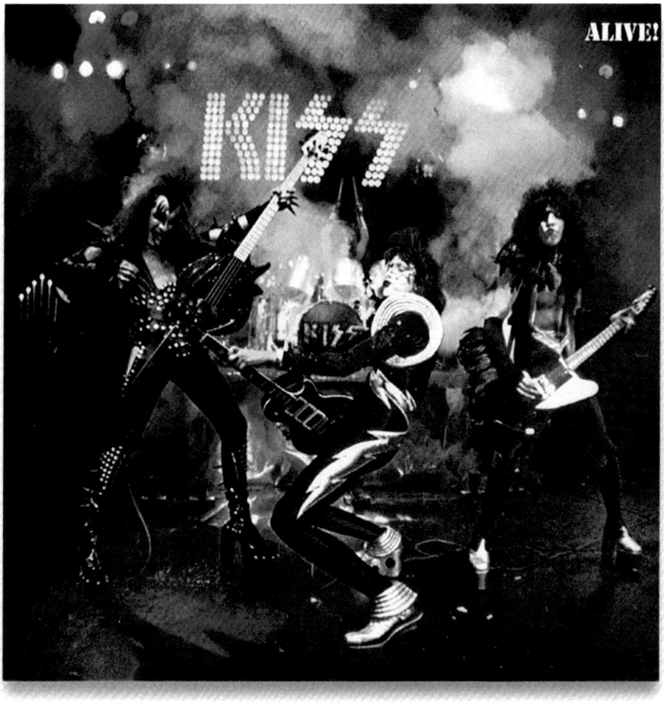

Left: The game changer. The success of *Alive!* pulled the band, their manager, and their record company back from the edge of financial oblivion. *(Universal Music Enterprises / Mercury Records / Kiss Catalog Ltd)*

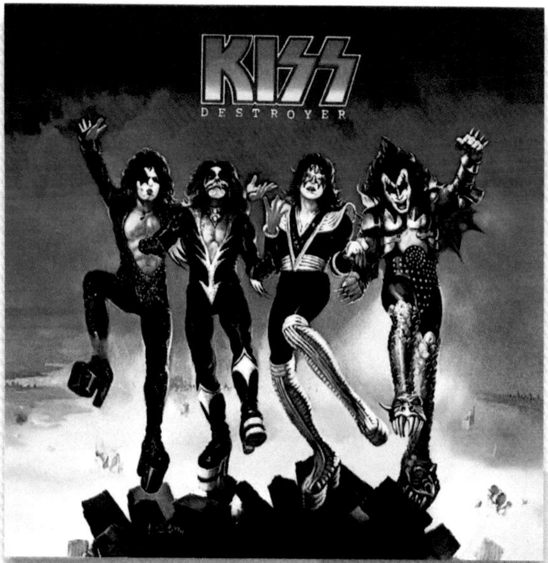

Left: *Destroyer* bettered *Alive!* in terms of sales and marked the band's transition from cult act to rock superstars. *(Universal Music Enterprises / Mercury Records / Kiss Catalog Ltd)*

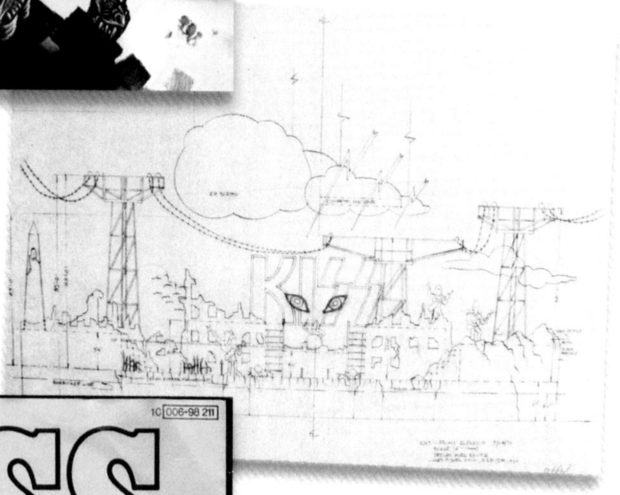

Right: Increased record sales meant increasingly elaborate stage sets. This blueprint of the *Destroyer* stage set was included in the 45th Anniversary Box Set *(Universal Music Enterprises / Kiss Catalog Ltd)*

Left: The German cover of the 'Detroit Rock City' single, which reached 14 on the West German chart, the only country in which it was a hit. *(Casablanca / EMI Electrola)*

Right: Ken Kelly's *Destroyer* art is one of the defining images of the band and has lent itself to a bewilderingly wide array of merchandise. *(Photograph by Joshua Gallagher)*

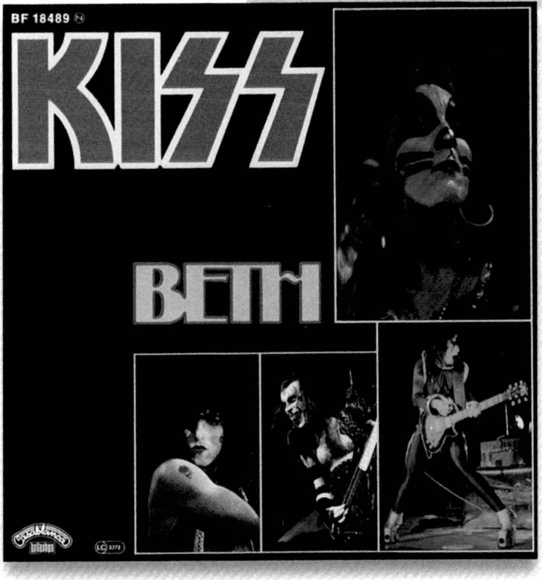

Left: The German cover of 'Beth'. Note the original Kiss logo remains intact; it was not banned in that country for its similarity to the SS symbol until 1979 – 1980. *(Casablanca / Bellaphon)*

Left: *Rock and Roll Over* featured another carefully crafted cover – this time by Michael Doret – that was ready-made for merchandising. *(Universal Music Enterprises / Mercury Records / Kiss Catalog Ltd)*

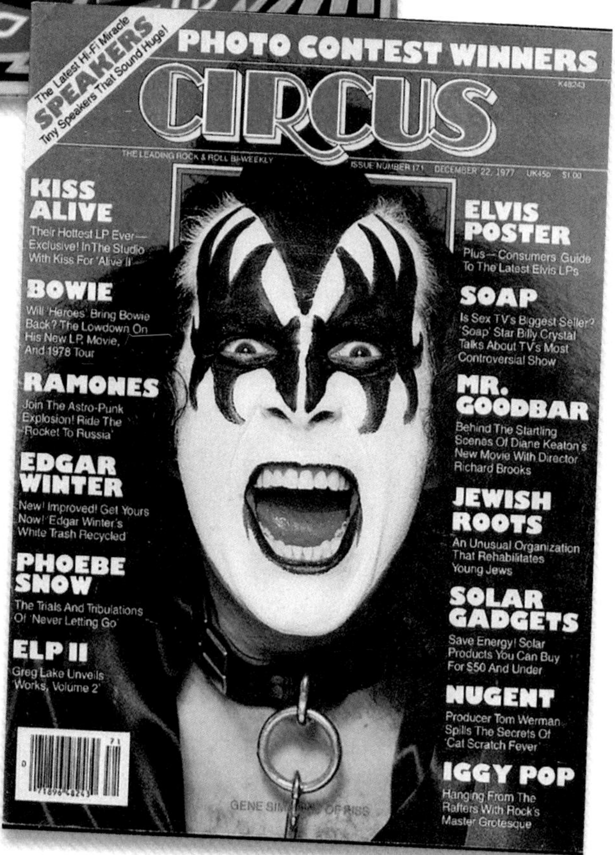

Right: Kiss became regular cover stars in the teen and music press, but the fact that Simmons featured predominantly, as in this December 1977 *Circus* cover, was a source of resentment to the other band members. *(flickr.com)*

Right: Ken Kelly returns to paint the cover for *Love Gun*, with his wife Rose serving as the model for all the women reclining at Kiss's feet. *(Universal Music Enterprises / Mercury Records / Kiss Catalog Ltd)*

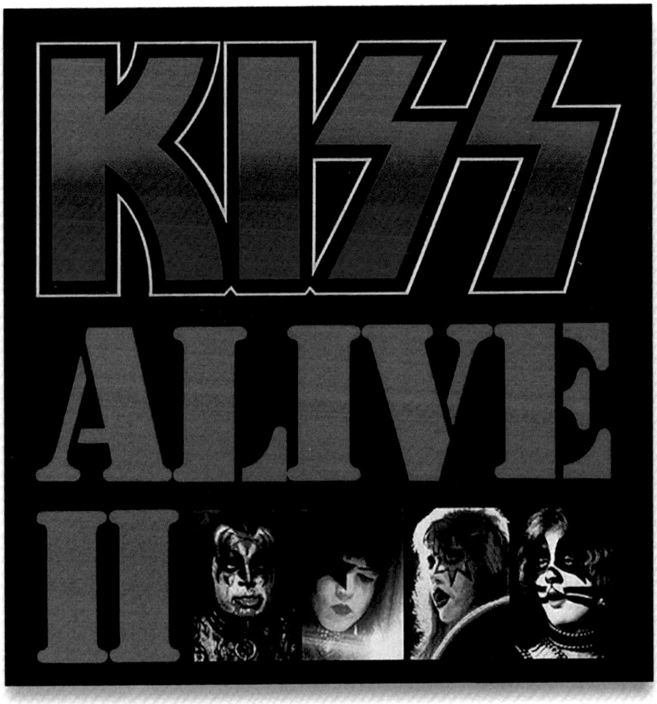

Left: To avoid repetition of material from the first live album, *Alive II* only featured songs from *Destroyer*, *Rock and Roll Over*, and *Love Gun*, plus a side of new studio tracks. *(Universal Music Enterprises / Mercury Records / Kiss Catalog Ltd)*

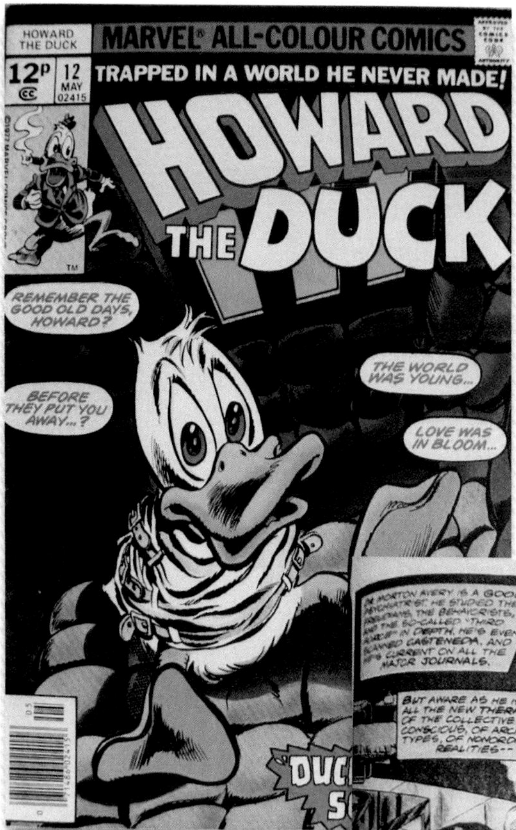

Left: The cover to *Howard the Duck* issue 12. This might seem a strange place for Kiss to make their comic book debut, but for Howard's creator Steve Gerber, 'strange' was just another day at the office. Photo by Joshua Gallagher. *(Marvel Entertainment)*

Right: Kiss appears on the final page of *Howard the Duck* 12, rendered by the art team of penciler Gene Colan and inker Steve Leiahola. Photo by Joshua Gallagher. *(Marvel Entertainment)*

Right: The 'Duck' issues were just a prelude to *Marvel Comics Super Special* 1 (1977), where Kiss makes the leap from rock stars to superheroes. The cover is by Alan Weiss and Gray Morrow. Photo by Joshua Gallagher. *(Marvel Entertainment)*

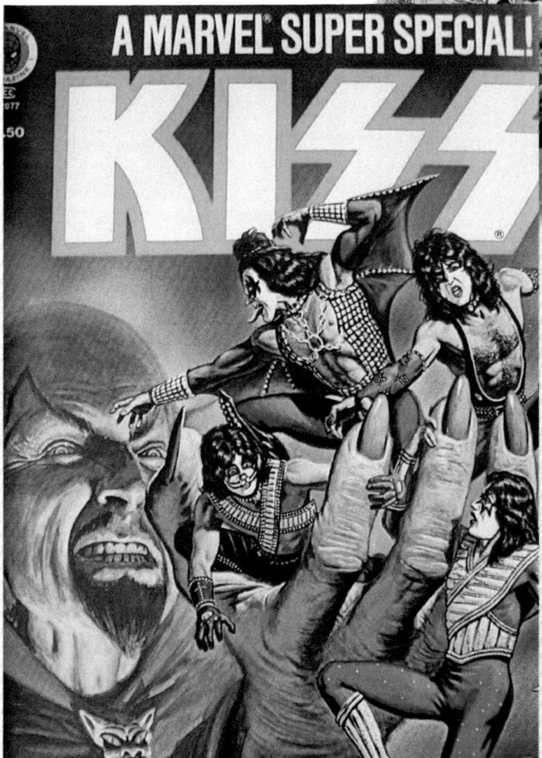

Left: The following year's *Marvel Comics Super Special* 5, with cover art by Bob Larkin, would be Kiss's last comic book caper until the original members reunited in the mid-nineties. Photo by Joshua Gallagher. *(Marvel Entertainment)*

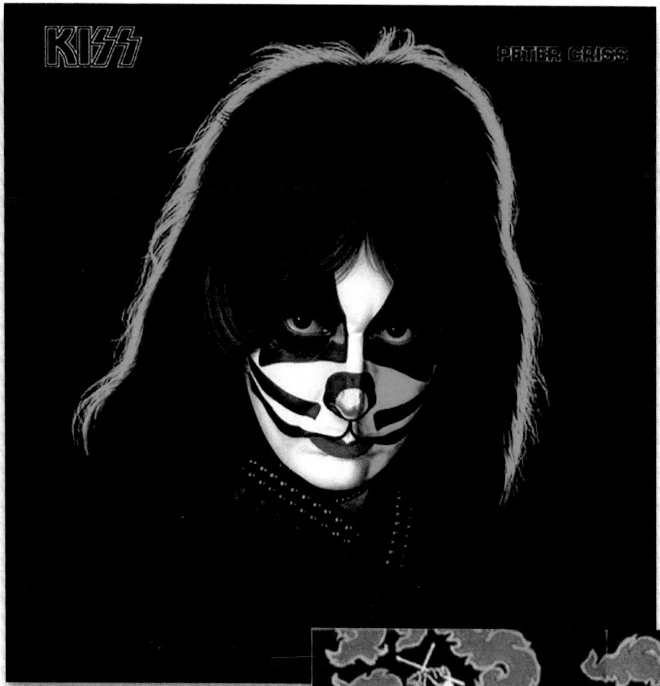

This page: *Peter Criss* solo album cover and poster insert. *(Universal Music Enterprises / Mercury Records / Kiss Catalog Ltd)*

This page: *Ace Frehley* solo album cover and poster insert. *(Universal Music Enterprises / Mercury Records / Kiss Catalog Ltd)*

Left: *Common One* illustrated a new direction, drawing on free jazz, but critics didn't understand, at least until Laster Bangs re-evaluated it as 'holy music' in 1982. (*Mercury/Warner/ Polydor*)

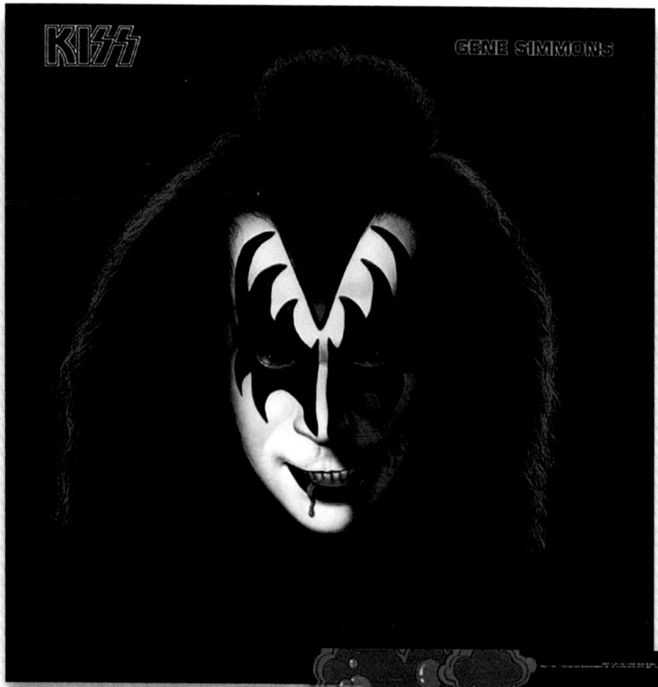

This page: *Gene Simmons* solo album cover and poster insert. *(Universal Music Enterprises / Mercury Records / Kiss Catalog Ltd)*

This page: *Paul Stanley* solo album cover and poster insert. *(Universal Music Enterprises / Mercury Records / Kiss Catalog Ltd)*

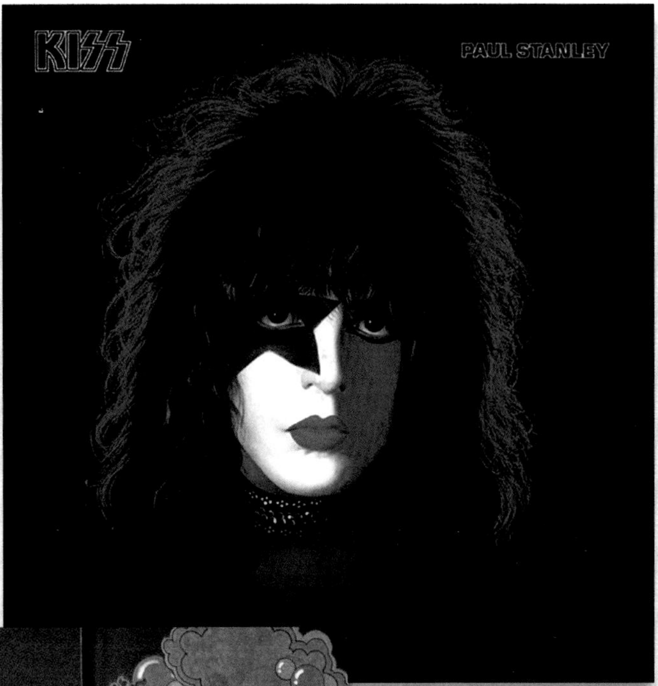

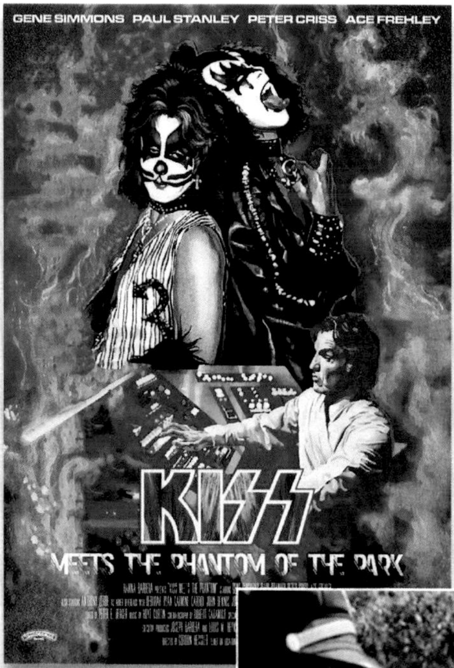

Left: The VHS cover of *Kiss Meets the Phantom of the Park*. *(Hanna-Barbera Productions / Warner Bros. / Kiss Catalog Ltd)*

Below: Gene consoles his fellow *Kiss Meets the Phantom of the Park* cast members: 'But just think, fellas. Thanks to us, *Plan 9 from Outer Space* is no longer the worst movie of all time'. *(Hanna-Barbera Productions / Warner Bros. / Kiss Catalog Ltd)*

Left: Executive producer Joseph Barbera thought *Kiss Meets the Phantom of the Park* was 'a terrific picture'. No one in this movie still agrees with him. *(Hanna-Barbera Productions / Warner Bros. / Kiss Catalog Ltd)*

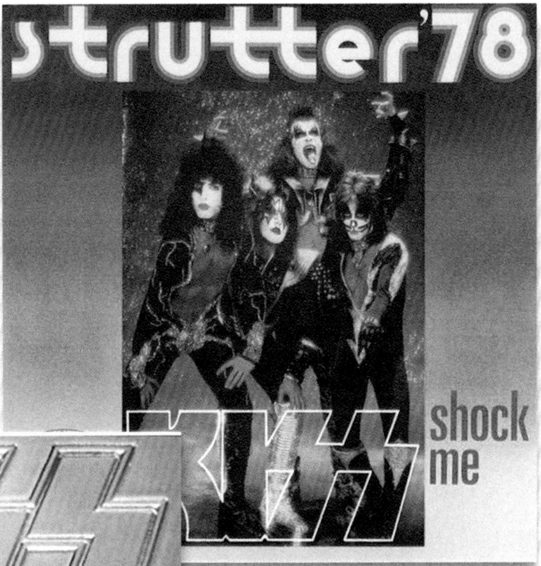

Right: The cover to the French release of the 'Strutter '78' single. Despite the involvement of Raspberries' producer Jimmy Lenner, it didn't differ significantly from the original version. *(Universal Music Enterprises / Mercury Records / Kiss Catalog Ltd)*

Left: *Double Platinum* was Kiss's first 'greatest hits' package. Its sleek, shiny, and subtle cover was the first not to feature the band's most marketable asset, their faces. *(Universal Music Enterprises / Mercury Records / Kiss Catalog Ltd)*

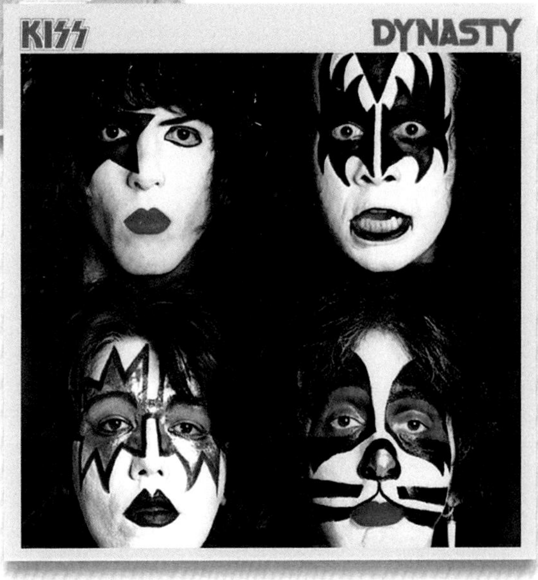

Right: The *Dynasty* cover presents an image of closeness and unity, but relationships within the band were at an all-time low. *(Universal Music Enterprises / Mercury Records / Kiss Catalog Ltd)*

Left: This German edition of *Unmasked* features the alternative logo that replaced the offending SS lightning bolts with backwards zeds. *(Universal Music Enterprises / Mercury Records / Kiss Catalog Ltd)*

Right: Thanks to merchandise leaflets such as this, which were included in albums from *Rock and Roll Over* onward, Kiss went from band to brand. *(Universal Music Enterprises / Mercury Records / Kiss Catalog Ltd)*

who had produced a successful run of albums for Aerosmith (*Get Your Wings*, *Toys in the Attic* and *Rocks*), and who had just completed production on the debut of another band managed by Bill Aucoin, Starz. However, Douglas was friends with Ezrin and passed. Kramer it was, then.

The new album, to be called *Rock and Roll Over*, was recorded over September and October at the Star Theatre, Nanuet, NY, a shuttered venue that had been partly owned by Criss's hero, Frank Sinatra. To emulate the band's live sound, the three guitarists performed and were recorded in the theatre itself, while Criss set up his kit in the bathroom in an attempt to get a fuller, beefier drum sound far removed from the tinniness that plagued the first three albums. He communicated with the rest of the band, and Kramer, via a video feed.

On 29 October, Kiss made their first prime-time network appearance when they appeared on *The Paul Lynde Halloween Special*. Lynde was a popular television actor, comedian, and game show panellist, best known for his role as Uncle Arthur in the sitcom *Bewitched*, and as the regular centre square on *Hollywood Squares*. He was also a voice artist for Hanna-Barbera cartoons and, although not produced by Hanna-Barbera, his *Halloween Special* plays out like a live-action version of their shows, with the camp ramped to the max. It is a stout heart that can watch it now without cringing, and it is difficult to imagine it was any easier to digest back then. Nonetheless, it was a significant career move for Kiss, as it introduced them to a wider audience, many of whom became fans.

Kiss performed three tracks from *Destroyer*, a truncated but frenetic 'Detroit Rock City', 'King of the Night Time World', also shortened, and 'Beth'. For this last named, Criss performed solo at a piano, the camera careful never to show his resolutely non-piano playing hands. At the song's conclusion, the three other members of Kiss appear around the piano, and Simmons places a consoling hand on Criss's shoulder, as if to reassure him he has made it through his ordeal. Gene should really have saved his comforting touch for the viewer, for the suffering was all theirs.

Kiss look beyond bored in their interactions with their host, but according to the *Destroyer 45th Anniversary Deluxe* box set book, they loved appearing on the show, not least because one of the other guests was Margaret Hamilton, reprising her role as the Wicked Witch from *The Wizard of Oz*. Simmons remembers, 'There are photos where I am sitting next to her. I wasn't just happy; it was beyond that. I was awed'. Frehley was similarly impressed. 'Meeting Margaret Hamilton was a real kick.

She was really sweet and friendly and so was everybody else. I grew up loving *The Wizard of Oz*, so it was cool to meet her.' Criss also recalls that his mother was thrilled he was appearing on the show, as Lynde was her favourite comedian.

Rock and Roll Over was released on 11 November and sported a cover every bit as classy as Ken Kelly's *Destroyer* painting. Casablanca art director Dennis Woloch knew he wanted something different for the new album and was thinking in terms of flat, bright colours and hard edges. He also had a notion for something circular to reflect the 'roll over' part of the album's title. He contacted Michael Doret, who was primarily a designer and lettering/logo artist rather than an illustrator, but whose work Woloch had admired. Doret had never heard of Kiss, so was given a quick primer on their stage characters and then set to work. Doret's initial idea was a composite image of the band, which Woloch nixed as unlikely to appeal to the band members' newly puffed-up egos and as being too close conceptually to the back cover of *Hotter Than Hell*. Doret's other idea, a circular image that could be viewed whichever way you turned it, got the thumbs up, although Woloch insisted that Gene and Paul appear in the top half of the cover.

Most of Doret's first draft made it to the final cover; the colour scheme, the Kiss logos occupying each corner of the cover, the circular saw containing the album title, three of the band members' backgrounds, all of Peter Criss's face, and much of Frehley's and Simmons'. The biggest changes were made to Stanley's face, which in the original sported a tight afro that made his whole face look squatter. He also had a nose like Simmons' on the finished version (as did Frehley) and lips in an ugly stylised heart design, all of which made for a very unflattering portrait. No one would have wanted this guy for a Lover. Doret made the required alterations, including some smaller changes to Ace and Gene's images and a repositioning of the album title, and the cover was done.

Doret's later work includes designing a fruit and vegetables stamp series for the United States Postal Service, creating the cover lettering for Taschen's monolithic *75 Years of DC Comics* and the logos for the New York Knicks and Disney's *Wreck-It Ralph*, and, in 2009, another Kiss cover, *Sonic Boom*.

Rock and Roll Over came with a sticker set reproducing the cover that was divided into sections, and such inserts were to be a feature of Kiss albums for the remainder of the 1970s. More significantly, it came with a merchandising leaflet, enticing the Kiss fan with such goodies as t-shirts, belt buckles, a foil poster of the *Destroyer* cover ('It's Hot!'), a Kiss photo set, a *Rock and Roll Over* button, and tour and song books. The band's transition into a brand was well underway.

The album starts strongly with 'I Want You'. A gentle acoustic melody opens the track with some sweet singing from Stanley, but this lasts all of fifteen seconds before the full band come in in blistering if-the-Stones-were-power-pop fashion. 'I Want You' features two back-to-back guitar solos, the first from Paul and the second from Ace, which winds down nicely to reintroduce the acoustic opening. However, now is as good a time as any to ask the question: why were all Kiss guitar solos so brief? Case in point, Stanley's solo here lasts all of ten seconds, and Frehley's only double that. Considering how short their average song was, and indeed their average album, extended solos could have fleshed out both without overstaying their welcome and would have given room for Frehley to better showcase his ability.

The lyrics are occasionally trippy ('You can live in a dream / And life will pass you by'), but at least they remain innuendo-free. That won't last long.

'Take Me' is also free of innuendo, but only because subtlety, and Ezrin's plea to stretch themselves lyrically, was thrown out the window. Exhibit A, the opening line of 'Take Me': 'Put your hands in my pocket /Grab onto my rocket'. Sean Delaney was drafted in to cowrite as Stanley was struggling with writer's block, which, going by what they came up with, turned out to be infectious. Shame, because, musically, Stanley once again nailed that Stones/power pop hybrid.

'Calling Dr. Love' began life as 'Bad, Bad Lovin'' which Simmons demoed in preparation for *Destroyer*, but he changed the lyrics after being inspired by the recurring dispatcher line 'Calling Doctor Howard, Doctor Fine, Doctor Howard' from the Three Stooges' 1934 short *Men in Black.* The song has a nice riff 'n' cowbell opening that introduces us to the medical profession's most lecherous practitioner. Simmons lurches into full-blown misogynistic egotism throughout but does at least conjure up a classic pop line in 'Baby, I know what your problem is / The first step of the cure is... A kiss'. 'Calling Dr. Love' has a typically short but seismic solo from Frehley, some solid drumming from Criss, who on this evidence at least seems to be the only one that took anything away from working with Ezrin, and comes with an undeniably catchy chorus, which no doubt helped propel it to numbers sixteen and two in the *Billboard* and Canadian charts respectively.

Simmons decided it was his turn to go all Stonsey with 'Ladies Room', but predictably it soon descends into another cock-rocker laced with cowbell and misogyny. 'Meet, meet you in the ladies room...'. What is wrong with this man? And – lord above – did fifteen-year-old American boys think this was cool?

As with 'Beth', Criss brought in another Stan Penridge co-write from a previous group and once again it concerns a bandmate, this time Lips bassist Michael Benvenga and his recently acquired automobile. 'Baby Driver' is a rocker that starts well, but it all too quickly goes into repeat mode, making it clear this is more an idea than an actual song. In a failed attempt to distract the listener from this, or perhaps in an equally unsuccessful bid to add some sort of excitement, Criss decides to stop singing and start screeching. The needle lifting from the vinyl at the end of this track comes as blessed relief.

Side two opens with a tune that was originally called 'Rock and Rolls Royce', a title that wonderfully predicts the so-bad-it's-goodness of Spinal Tap. Sadly, Simmons opted to retitle this *Destroyer* cast-off 'Love 'Em, Leave 'Em', another interminable ode to groupies wrapped up in a toe-tappin' toon. In other words, it's 'Room Service'. Or 'Ladies in Waiting'. Again.

'Mr. Speed', another Stanley-Delaney cowrite, cranks the Jagger swagger to max and again demonstrates Stanley's ear for a good hook. Surprisingly, it never featured on the concert setlist, perhaps because someone pointed out that it sounds like Paul's bragging about being a premature ejaculator and that, buddy, is one boast you might wanna keep to yourself.

'See You in Your Dreams' is Simmons' final composition on *Rock and Roll Over* and, with 'Calling Dr. Love', is a contender for his best contribution. Although it is never a genre Kiss ever identified with, it shows that Gene too could pull a top power pop tune out of his bag if required, and it features sterling work from both Criss and Frehley.

'Hard Luck Woman', a Stanley solo effort that uncharacteristically featured him on twelve-string acoustic guitar and Frehley on a six-string acoustic, took as its lyrical inspiration the 1972 number one hit 'Brandy' by Looking Glass, who would eventually evolve into Starz. Musically, it was written with Rod Stewart in mind, and Stanley entertained hopes of pitching it to the British singer, but Kramer and Simmons insisted that Criss sing the song and that it be the follow-up single to 'Beth'. They were right; released as a precursor to the album on 1 November, it reached number 15 in both the *Billboard* and Canadian charts.

Rock and Roll Over concludes satisfyingly with the furious riffing of 'Makin' Love', a proto thrash metaller supported by a simple but surprisingly supple bass line that never strays from the top two strings and is, along with 'Hard Luck Woman', one of two Stanley songs on the album that doesn't betray an obvious Stones influence. According to Stanley in *Behind the Mask*, ''Makin' Love' was a tip of the hat to Led Zeppelin's 'Whole Lotta Love''.

If the band's intention was indeed to return to their basic rock and roll roots whilst producing an album that banished the weedy production that dogged their first three long players, then *Rock and Roll Over* was a triumph. It was also a commercial success, spending forty-seven weeks on the *Billboard* chart, peaking, like its predecessor, at eleven. It also enjoyed significant chart action in Australia, Canada, Japan, and Sweden. It was released on 11 November, the same day that *Destroyer* became the band's first platinum record.

Rock and Roll Over got a favourable(ish) review from a surprising quarter. Max Bell, writing in the usually dismissive *NME,* opined that 'Soon it will be time for Kiss to fall into the so-bad-it's nearly-good category and most of the ditties herein fully deserve that compliment. Best rip-off is a piss-take on Rod Stewart, 'Hard Luck Woman', which is superb'. Over in the usually supportive *Circus*, Lester Bangs no doubt spoke for many: 'I am sick of those guys' *weltanschaung*; they should stop singing about fucking, which is nobody else's business anyway'.

A new album meant a new tour, so the *Rock and Roll Over* tour began on 24 November, just over two months after the *Destroyer* tour ended, and would run through to 4 April 1977. A variety of acts opened for Kiss, the most frequent being Uriah Heep, who joined the tour on 8 December. This was the concert debut of both John Lawton and Trevor Bolder.

The year ended in electrifying fashion, at least for Ace Frehley, who was electrocuted on stage at the December 12 show at Lakeland Civic Centre, Florida. While coming down the staircase that formed part of the stage set during show opener 'Detroit Rock City', his guitar touched the non-grounded railing, and he was thrown back and briefly lost consciousness. When they realised what had happened, the other three members stopped the show. After a break of five to ten minutes, and despite having burns on his fingers, Frehley felt fit enough to go back on stage, where he was greeted with a standing ovation. As if determined not to be outshone, Simmons later set his hair alight. Again.

1977: Marvel Comics, Love Gun, and Alive II

Love Gun

Personnel:
Paul Stanley: rhythm guitar, vocals
Ace Frehley: lead guitar, vocals
Gene Simmons: bass, vocals
Peter Criss: drums, vocals
Additional personnel:
Eddie Kramer: Keyboards on 'Christine Sixteen', 'I Stole Your Love', and 'Love Gun'
Jimmy Maelen: Congas on 'Almost Human'
Tasha Thomas, Ray Simpson, and Hilda Harris: backing vocals on 'Tomorrow and Tonight'
Recorded at the Record Plant, New York City, May 1977
Produced by Kiss and Eddie Kramer
Released: 30 June 1977
Running time: 32.53
Highest chart place: 4 (US)
Tracklisting: 1. 'I Stole Your Love' (Stanley) 3.04, 2. 'Christine Sixteen' (Simmons) 3.14, 3. 'Got Love for Sale' (Simmons) 3.29, 4. 'Shock Me' (Frehley) 3.49, 5. 'Tomorrow and Tonight' (Stanley) 3.40, 6. 'Love Gun' (Stanley) 3.18, 7. 'Hooligan' (Criss, Penridge) 3.01, 8. 'Almost Human' (Simmons) 2.49, 9. 'Plaster Caster' (Simmons) 3.27, 10. 'Then She Kissed Me' (Barry, Greenwich, Spector) 3.02

Alive II

Personnel:
Paul Stanley: rhythm guitar, vocals
Ace Frehley: lead guitar, vocals
Gene Simmons: bass, vocals
Peter Criss: drums, vocals
Recorded at the Forum, Los Angeles 26-28 August 1977 with additional recording at Capitol Theatre, Passaic, New Jersey, and Budokan Hall, Tokyo
Studio side recorded at Electric Lady Studio, New York City, 13-16 September 1977
Produced by Eddie Kramer and Kiss
Released: 24 October 1977
Running time: 71.26
Highest chart places: US: 7, UK: 60
Tracklisting: 1. 'Detroit Rock City' (Stanley, Ezrin) 3.58, 2. 'King of the Night Time World' (Stanley, Ezrin, Fowley, Anthony) 3.06, 3. 'Ladies Room' (Simmons) 3.11, 4.

'Makin' Love' (Stanely, Delaney) 3.13, 5. 'Love Gun' (Stanley) 3.34, 6. 'Calling Dr. Love' (Simmons) 3.32, 7. 'Christine Sixteen' (Simmons) 2.45, 8. 'Shock Me' (Frehley) 5.51, 9. 'Hard Luck Woman' (Stanley) 3.06, 10. 'Tomorrow and Tonight' (Stanley) 3.20, 11. 'I Stole Your Love' (Stanley) 3.36, 12. 'Beth' (Criss, Penridge, Ezrin) 2.24, 13. 'God of Thunder[' (Stanley) 5.16, 14. 'I Want You' (Stanley) 4.14, 15. 'Shout It Out Loud' (Stanley, Simmons, Ezrin) 3.37, 16. 'All American Man' (Stanley, Delaney) 3.13, 17. 'Rockin' in the U.S.A.' (Simmons) 2.38, 18. 'Larger Than Life' (Simmons) 3.55, 19. 'Rocket Ride' (Frehley, Delaney) 4.07, 20. 'Any Way You Want It' (Clark) 2.33

Despite the obvious triumphs of 1976, Kiss's newfound success was taking its toll, and fissures were appearing, as these snippets from Criss, Stanley, and Frehley's autobiographies make clear.

Criss: 'Slowly but surely, I became addicted to cocaine. I got crazier and crazier. I capitalised on the fact I was in the hottest band in the world and I could get away with anything. I acted out, in part, because I was beginning to feel so alienated from Gene and Paul that I just didn't want to be around them anymore. The joy of making music with them was gone'.

Stanley: 'There was very little band mentality anymore. The other three guys drifted off to their own social circles, and we all had our own people telling each of us how great we were. Both Peter and Ace were fucked up all the time. The situation made me angry. I had busted my ass for the band, and I felt that these two guys were playing fast and loose with my future based on their irrational whims and inner conflicts'.

Frehley, who had one co-write on *Destroyer* and none on *Rock and Roll Over*: 'I started feeling uncreative and unfulfilled. I started feeling like a caricature. More than once, when Kiss was at the height of its popularity, I found myself sitting in my dressing room, staring into a mirror and shaking my head at the sight of the Spaceman. Kiss was no longer a dream job. It was merely a job'.

As the *Rock and Roll Over* Tour juggernauted across North America, the band made an unheralded appearance in a most unlikely place, issue 12 of Marvel's *Howard the Duck* comic book, which, although cover-dated May 1977, would have appeared on newsstands and spinner racks sometime in February. Howard, a sarcastic, cigar-chomping duck from another dimension, was the creation and on-page alter-ego of Steve Gerber, arguably the most interesting and innovative comic book writer of the 1970s. In this issue, Howard had been committed to a psychiatric hospital where he meets a new acquaintance, Winda Wester, who claims to be possessed. The last page, depicting a familiar black and white-faced foursome billowing forth from Winda's skull, suggests she wasn't kidding.

The story continues in issue 13, and after two pages of mayhem ably illustrated by artists Gene Colan and Steve Leialoha, Peter Criss whispers in Howard's ear, 'When you meet reality head on – kiss it, smack in the face! That's the word! Pass it on!' Message delivered, the four apparitions disappear back into Winda's brain. Later, the whole incident is explained away as 'an unusual phenomenon and very unlikely to recur'.

On the one hand, the use of Kiss in Howard's tale was typical of Gerber, whose appreciation for popular music often manifested in his stories. In the hundredth issue of *Daredevil*, again drawn by Colan, Gerber had the titular hero being interviewed by *Rolling Stone*'s Jann Wenner. Analogues of the Beatles, complete with a yellow submarine, appeared in his *Sub-Mariner* run. However, this time out Kiss's appearance in *Howard the Duck* seemed completely gratuitous, their only purpose seemingly a plot contrivance to later introduce another established Marvel character. In fact, it was a harbinger of an altogether more ambitious project.

Sometime in 1976, Bill Aucoin had approached Marvel about doing a comic book featuring the band. Stan Lee, nominal publisher and public face of the company, was excited about the idea and tapped Gerber as writer. Gerber had no real knowledge of Kiss outside of admiring their logo on t-shirts but was as enthusiastic as Lee, having long believed that Marvel should expand into the rock music field. How he felt about Sean Delaney's insistence that the band be depicted as superheroes instead of musicians is not recorded, but Gerber firmly backed Rock Steady's assertion that the project be a dollar-fifty magazine rather than a standard comic book. Gerber had previously worked in advertising and, 'As he saw it', writes Sean Howe in his excellent *Marvel Comics: The Untold Story*, 'high-quality colour comic magazines were a way out of the industry free fall – getting Marvel out of the advertising ghetto of Sea Monkeys and X-Ray Spex and You Too Can Draw Timmy the Turtle, appealing to real Madison Advertisers like respectable periodicals did'. Gerber was flown to a Kiss show, met with the band, and, crucially, got on with them well, especially Gene, no doubt because they were both Jewish comic book nerds at heart. The project was on.

And then it was nearly off, due to hubris on an unthinkable scale on the part of Marvel's management (not Lee, who had creative influence but no say in financial matters). Fortunately, Gerber, famous for writing unorthodox heroes, briefly became one himself. Here's Mary Skrenes, Gerber's partner at the time, interviewed by George Khoury for his book *Comic Book Fever: A Celebration of Comics 1976-1986*:

> Steve came to me, white and shaking. He told me that the Marvel publishers did not want to put out a book with characters that they didn't own. They really had no idea who or what Kiss was. They thought they could put out their own rock 'n' roll superhero book and own the characters and cash in whatever piddling market there was. And graciously, Steve could still write the book.
>
> Steve was horrified. No contracts had been signed yet, but this was breaking an explicit trust. He could never be party to something like that. He knew his career was over because if he didn't go along, he would be blackballed.
>
> He asked me what to do. I hesitated for a moment because I knew this was a seminal moment in his life. But for a man of his character, there was only one answer.

Gerber went to Aucoin and told him what was afoot. Even though Marvel's management would quickly work out that Gerber was the whistle-blower, Skrenes remembers that his primary concern was for Lee, who would be blamed for Gerber's perceived lack of loyalty. In the end, Aucoin's legal team 'scared the shit out of Marvel' (Skrenes's words), and contracts were signed, with one stipulation being that Gerber remained as writer.

From Howard the Duck to 'Disco Duck'. This novelty number by Rick Dees and His Cast of Idiots was nominated, along with 'Muskrat Love' by the Captain and Tennille and 'Beth', for the People's Choice Award for the Best Song of 1976, a selection that surely suggests only three singles were released in the bicentennial year. At the award ceremony on 10 February, 'Beth' had to share the gong with 'Disco Duck'. Kiss were performing in Chicago that night, so Lydia Criss accepted on behalf of the band. Kiss received a further accolade on 28 February when *Dressed to Kill* was certified gold.

For Kiss, the highlight of the *Rock and Roll Over* tour, indeed the highlight of their career to date, occurred on 18 February, when they played a sold-out show at Madison Square Garden. Stanley dreamed of this moment since, as a cabbie in 1972, he had dropped off people going to see Elvis at the Garden, and now it was his turn. It was a moment of victory and vindication and a homecoming; the band's families were all in the audience. Criss recalls being so stressed out he threw up twice before taking the stage; Stanley took half a Valium to calm his nerves. The critics were savage, but for the band and their ecstatic fans, it was a triumph. But it was only a teaser trailer for the reception they would receive in Japan, when the band toured there for the first time in March and April.

They landed in Tokyo on 19 March, having made the flight in a Pan-Am Clipper adorned with the Kiss logo (according to Chris Lendt in *Kiss and Sell*, this led Criss to believe the band owned the airplane). As they had done in England, Kiss disembarked in full make-up to meet the press. Unlike in England, they were met by thousands of adoring fans screaming for their idols. It was Kissteria, the Seventies' version of the previous decade's Beatlemania. Not even having to take their makeup off again to prove to customs that they really were the people in their passport photos could dampen the mood.

Kiss played ten shows in Japan, culminating in four dates at the famed Budokan arena. The matinee and evening shows on 2 April were recorded by Eddie Kramer, intended for a Japan-only live album provisionally titled *A Rock and Roll Party in Tokyo*. It remains unreleased.

Kiss returned to the States on 5 April and had the rest of the month off, reconvening on 3 May to record *Love Gun* at the Record Plant, NYC, with Kramer again producing. Recording continued to the end of the month. On 13 May, the band were measured for their new Love Gun costumes, which were designed by Laurie Greenan, who worked with the band through to the end of the makeup years. She later styled stage outfits for Todd Rundgren, Billy Idol, Judas Priest, and, surprisingly, Tom Waits.

Now that Greenan's costume designs had been revealed, art director Dennis Woloch could start thinking about the album cover. Although he thought it too soon to reuse Ken Kelly, both Aucoin and Kiss business manager Howard Marks were pushing him to do so as his *Destroyer* painting had given them such a marketable image. Woloch and Kelly's initial concept had the band emerging from the stage door of a grimy New York theatre to a group of female fans, but this was swiftly knocked back, Simmons for one thinking the band were now bigger than the image being projected. Kelly went back to the drawing board, using himself as the model for the band members and his wife Rose for all the women scattered at Kiss's feet, changing Kiss from club band to rock and roll Olympians, and giving them a more palatial setting. Ever modest, the band deemed this image acceptable. This would be Kelly's last work for Kiss, although he would paint a variation of the first-ever *Fantastic Four* cover for Marvel's 1996 comic *Kissnation* and render the cover of Frehley's 2014 solo outing *Space Invader*. He died in June 2022, and Criss, Simmons, and Stanley all paid tribute on social media.

On 26 May, Kiss took a day off recording and flew to a printing plant in Buffalo in the company of Stan Lee. There, in a publicity stunt orchestrated by Aucoin, each band member had some blood drawn by a registered nurse, and this was then mixed with the red ink that would be used in printing the Kiss comic. A long-standing rumour, believed to have originated with Bill Aucoin, has it that an error at the printing plant led to the blood being used in an issue of *Sports Illustrated*.

Another persistent rumour stemming from this period is that Kiss had knocked back the opportunity to appear in the movie *Rollercoaster*, which opened on 10 June. It seems unlikely that Aucoin, who happily signed the band up for the Paul Lynde show and the Marvel comic, would deny his charges their first opportunity to appear on the big screen, and when asked later, Simmons claims to have never even heard of the movie. The part went to Sparks, who subsequently hailed their appearance in the film as one of their biggest regrets. *Rollercoaster* was largely filmed at Magic Mountain amusement park in Valencia, California, which coincidentally would also provide the setting when Kiss did make their movie debut the following year.

June would prove to be a very successful month for Kiss, with their debut album and *Hotter Than Hell* both being certified gold and the band coming first in an America's Top Band Gallup poll. The month ended with the release of *Love Gun*.

The album opens in fine style with 'I Stole Your Love' (or 'Ah Thtole Yo Luv', as Stanley styles it), a metallic-edged pop song played at a breakneck pace. It features some nice drum work from Criss, particularly his use of the floor tom. Stanley called it 'a sister song' to the title track and says it was influenced by Deep Purple's 'Burn'.

'Christine Sixteen' sees Simmons back in the old perv mode first demonstrated on 'Goin' Blind', here lurking outside the school gates infatuated with the title character. The title originated with Stanley, with Simmons beating him to the punch in writing the song. Eddie Kramer played the piano, and then unknowns Eddie and Alex Van Halen played guitar and drums respectively on the demo, with Frehley essentially copying Van Halen's lead on the finished track. The talking part was inspired by old doo-wop records.

'Christine Sixteen' was released as the first single from *Love Gun* and did well in North America, despite not being played on some radio stations because of its lyrics. It reached 25 on the *Billboard* chart and 22 in Canada.

'Got Love for Sale' is a punchy number but with nothing new to offer. Be it Simmons' by now standard and tiresome egotism or Frehley's phoned-in solo, it all sounds like something that's been heard before. Once again, Eddie and Alex Van Halen played on the demo.

'Shock Me' is Frehley's first solo writing credit since 'Getaway' on *Dressed to Kill*, and his first stab at lead vocals, which he famously sang lying on his back on the studio floor to overcome his nerves. He was never going to unseat Stanley as Kiss's best vocalist, but his unmistakable Bronx accent only adds charm. His fifty-second guitar solo is his longest to date and remains one of his best. Criss also steps up, filling the spaces with lots of great little drum fills. The lyrics were very, very loosely inspired by his on-stage electrocution the previous December.

Side one closer, 'Tomorrow and Tonight' was inspired by Mott the Hoople's 'Golden Age of Rock and Roll' and, by Stanley's admission, an attempt to recapture 'Rock and Roll All Nite's lightning in a bottle. With Stanley's pop chops front and centre, it is arguably superior to the latter. No wonder he hollers joyfully at the end of the second chorus; he clearly knows this is a winner. Even those scoffing the risible 'Take it in the cel-lah / Let me be your fel-lah' clunker-couplet must surely succumb when the guitar solo ends to leave the Kissettes singing the chorus unaccompanied. Why it was never released as a single is a mystery. 'Tomorrow and Tonight' could, and should, have been part of the summer of seventy-seven's soundtrack.

For the record, the Kissettes were a one-song-only trio consisting of Tasha Thomas, Ray Simpson, and Hilda Harris. A couple of years after singing backing vocals here, Ray Simpson found fame when he took over the role of the Cop in the Village People, another Casablanca act.

At the time of its release, some musos in the English music press pondered whether the title 'Love Gun' might not be a sly nod to the Sex Pistols, but nope! It's about Paul Stanley's dick. 'A love gun', he told Wesley Strick of *Circus*, 'is the gun you're born with, that never comes off'. Hrrm. Try telling that to John Wayne Bobbitt.

Anyway, it is hardly an original idea. Compare this line from Booker T. and the M.G.'s 'The Hunter', 'Ain't no use to hide / Ain't no use to run / 'Cause I've got you in the sights of my love gun' with Stanley's 'No place for hiding, baby / No place to run / You pull the trigger of my love gun'. Add to this the guitar solo, possibly Frehley's best, but one which bears more than a passing resemblance to that on the Blue Magoos' 'We Ain't Got Nothin' Yet'. Despite these homages/plagiarisms, 'Love Gun' is a Kiss classic, a thrill ride in just over three minutes, and a concert staple since the record came out. Also, for the record, Stanley played the bass and all guitar parts except the solo.

'Hooligan' was the by now token Criss contribution, cowritten as ever with Stan Penridge. The original demo presented the song as a sloppy, bluesy number, which was hardly Kiss's thing, so it could not have come as a surprise that Stanley and Simmons rearranged it. This did not go down well with its creators, Criss stating in *Makeup to Breakup* that the song was 'butchered', and Penridge observing in *Behind the Mask* that 'The spontaneity and fun seemed to have been replaced with crunch and hype'. The best quote regarding this song, however, goes to engineer Corky Stasiak, also in *Behind the Mask*: 'Eddie was not happy with the original chorus, so Peter was writing the lyrics on the spot while we were recording. I came up with the line 'I'm a hooligan, won't to go to school again.'' How bad could the original have been if that was the acceptable replacement?

Criss and Penridge also proposed a song called 'Love Bite' (sample lyric: 'I've been bit everywhere / But I've never been bit by a woman there'), which Penridge suggests was knocked back for being 'too raunchy', but it is just as likely its name was too close to the title track to be used.

'Almost Human' sees the rhythm section getting almost funky, including session musician Jimmy Maelin on congas. Early indications suggest this number might be borderline cool, but then Simmons drowns everything out with his shouty singing 'style'. Thankfully, he reins his vocals in for 'Plaster Caster', a jaunty bop-along homage to Cynthia Albritton, a Sixties groupie famous for creating plaster casts of musicians' erect penises. Simmons was never one of Albritton's sitters, as she had effectively retired in the 1970s, nor was Jim Croce, who also referred to her in his 1973 song 'Five Short Minutes'.

Love Gun ends with 'Then She Kissed Me', a gender-reassigned take on the Crystals' 'Then He Kissed Me', and the band's first cover version since 'Kissin' Time' was foisted upon them as a single in 1974. It was Stanley's idea, but he has since been dismissive of it, saying, 'That's a great song and it needs to get redone like 'I Want to Hold Your Hand' needs to get redone', i.e., not at all. Inessential this glammed-up, fuzzy-guitar reconstruction of the Wall of Sound may be, but it is also perfectly enjoyable, with an enthusiastic vocal from Paul, who also supplies the lovely little 'do-bi-do' guitar solo.

Love Gun was Kiss's highest-charting album of the decade in their homeland, peaking at number four on the *Billboard* chart. It went one better north of the border, and hit the top twenty in Australia, Germany, and Sweden. As ever, the album's commercial success was at odds with its critical appraisal. *Rolling Stone*'s Charles M. Young wasted his word count making dick jokes before concluding by referring to the upcoming *Alive II*, saying 'that album will contain the definitive versions of everything potentially worth hearing on *Love Gun*'. Faint praise, indeed. The *NME*, in the person of Mick Farren, were as dismissive as ever, writing the album off as, 'a compendium of warmed-over rock clichés punctuated by largely redundant power chords'. Conversely, *Billboard* were *Love Gun* lovers, calling it Kiss's 'most flawlessly produced and written album yet.'

Harsh as Farren's assessment was, it was hard to disagree with. I was a fifteen-year-old fan when I bought *Love Gun* upon its release, and despite undeniable classics such as 'Shock Me', 'Tomorrow and Tonight', and the title cut, it was hard to think of the album as anything other than *Rock and Roll Over Volume 2*, which in turn was merely a better produced descendent of the first three platters. The great *Destroyer* experiment was only a year in the past, yet already it was looking like the band's lasting masterpiece. They were musically stagnating and lyrically stunted, their songs a ceaseless cycle about sex and ego and the occasional party, with few capable of reaching a third verse. Verse-chorus-verse-chorus-guitar solo-chorus-chorus-chorus-yadda-yadda-yadda *ad infinitum*.

Fortunately, *Love Gun* didn't need to involve active listening, as the *Kiss* comic was released as a Marvel Comics Super Special the same day, so the album could serve as the background music while reading the comic. The plot, such as it is, is this: Four young New Yorkers (you know their names) are transformed into super-powered weirdos by talismans within the Box Of Khyscz, which leads to a confrontation with Marvel Comics' big bad, Doctor Doom. After this inconclusive initial meeting, Paul and Gene take a trip to Hell and fight Satan-substitute Mephisto, while Ace and Peter arrive on a space station/disco. Why any of this happens is anyone's guess. The story concludes with a second, equally inconclusive meeting with Doom, where the supervillain lets the foursome keep the talismans but with the promise they haven't seen the last of him.

As stated earlier, Steve Gerber was a creative colossus, and at the absolute height of his powers in the mid-Seventies. His work on *Howard the Duck*, *Man-Thing*, *Omega the Unknown*, and *The Defenders* was like nothing seen in comics before and is still considered seminal today. Unfortunately, and despite the buck-fifty entry fee and the slick packaging, this 'Super Special' is possibly his least sophisticated story and looks like a rush job, a perception enhanced by the fact it took three different artists to produce the comic's forty pages, none of whom bring their top game. It didn't matter. Kiss were the 'hottest band in the land', so the comic shifted half a million copies, making it Marvel's best seller to date, a record it held until 1990. Of more lasting significance than the story is the fact that this Kiss comic book marks the first time Stanley's character is identified as the Starchild.

A new record meant a new tour, and the *Love Gun* Tour kicked off at Halifax, Nova Scotia, on 8 July. Cheap Trick were the support for most of the tour, with Styx taking over for the last four dates. The three shows at the Forum in Los Angeles, 26-28 August, were recorded for the band's second live platter, with 'I was there!' badges distributed to attendees. 'Firehouse', 'Rock and Roll All Nite', and 'Black Diamond' were all in the set list but were not used on *Alive II*, as the band didn't want tracks repeated over both live albums.

That meant using only live versions of songs culled from *Destroyer*, *Rock and Roll Over*, and *Love Gun*, but there were not enough tracks played during the tour to fill a double album. The solution was twofold: first, the band would record five new studio songs for side four of *Alive II*; and second, some songs from the previous three albums would be rerecorded and overdubbed with audience noise to give the illusion they were part of the concert. Regular Kiss engineer Corky Stasiak kept extensive diaries, and notes that 'Tomorrow and Tonight' was recorded in the studio on 13 September, the same day the new Simmons song 'Larger Than Life' was cut. Astonishingly, this pop diamond only made its true live debut forty years later, when it was played on the 2017 Kiss Kruise. Meanwhile, Julian Gill, creator of the bewilderingly detailed *Kiss Concert History Online* website, notes that 'King of the Night Time World' and 'Hard Luck Woman' were not played during the *Love Gun* tour, and suggests the *Alive II* versions of these songs were recorded during soundchecks for the Forum shows.

Alive II hit the stores on 14 October, wrapped up in a striking Dennis Woloch-designed sleeve, especially the eye-popping gatefold, a staged shot showcasing just about every effect at a Kiss concert going off at once. Included was the inevitable merchandising brochure, as well as an 'Evolution of Kiss' booklet and a set of tattoos. The first three sides feature deliriously pumped-up versions of the studio songs, none more so than 'God of Thunder', memorably described by Geoff Barton of *Sounds* as 'the vinyl equivalent of Armageddon'. The track directly preceding this is 'Beth,' which features Criss singing over a backing track of the original *Destroyer* version. This seems like a bit of a cheat; couldn't Stanley and/or Frehley have learned the song? The answer of course, is yes, as they did so in the *Kiss Meets the Phantom of the Park* television movie and the *MTV Unplugged* concert. The use of pre-recorded music on 'Beth' could lead a suspicious or cynical mind to the obvious question: what else have they used a backing track on?

'All American Man' by Stanley and Sean Delaney opens the studio side. 'I don't have any real connection to 'All American Man',' recalled Stanley in *Behind the Mask*. Perhaps this is because it originated from the same songwriting session that produced 'Take Me', 'Mr. Speed', and 'Makin' Love' for *Rock and Roll Over*, and they made the cut while 'All America Man' was shelved. From a lyrical point of view, it doesn't even make it to two verses, so sounds unfinished. Musically, however, what a difference a year makes. Kiss were often labelled hard rock, sometimes even heavy metal, but in truth, they were a plain ol' rock band. One only needs look at their influences: the Beatles, the Stones, the Who, the Move, the Small Faces, the Raspberries, and so on. On 'All American Man', the rock can justifiably be prefixed with 'hard', with dense, crunching guitars reminiscent of Bachman-Turner Overdrive.

Despite being in the building, Frehley was either disinterested or under the influence of something or other, so Bob Kulick, who had auditioned for Kiss back in 1973, played the lead guitar on this and 'Larger Than Life', and lead and rhythm on 'Rockin' in the U.S.A.'

'Rockin' in the U.S.A.' is a Simmons song whose general riffery is just a mite too close to other Simmons songs, for example, 'Got Love For Sale' from the previous album. If the lyrics were all about how much women wanted him, then this would be a perfect parody. Instead, they are all about how patriotic he is. When discussing this song in *Behind the Mask*, Simmons somehow thought quoting Ted Nugent would be a good idea. The quote was, essentially, 'Learn English or get the fuck out of America'. Although recognising this as an outrageously right-wing comment, Simmons concluded that, 'emotionally I think that's right'.

So, 'Rockin' in the U.S.A.' is 'Rock and Roll All Nite' for xenophobes and midnight cross-burners.

Simmons' second contribution, 'Larger Than Life', fares better. We are back in heavy territory, with some vaguely sinister riffing and some wonderful soloing where Kulick makes his guitar wail like the proverbial banshee. The lyrics are the usual letdown; you can probably guess what is larger than life (hint: not his ego, incredibly).

The standout of the studio cuts is 'Rocket Ride', a one-off collaboration between Frehley and Sean Delaney. It is the usual lyrical nonsense ('C'mon, grab a hold of my rocket!'), but has an arrangement more complex than the average Kiss song and, as with 'Shock Me', it allows Frehley some breathing room on his solos. Frehley played all the guitars on 'Rocket Ride', including bass, and Criss was behind the drumkit.

The second-best track of the studio set is the closer, a cover of the Dave Clark Five's 1964 hit 'Any Way You Want It'. As with 'Then She Kissed Me', Stanley has largely dismissed this but, as with the Crystals cover, this is a blocky, shlocky version with Stanley delivering that sleazy-rasp glam vocal he does so well. This Dave Clark-penned tune obviously had its fans as, in 1996, the Ramones chose to close their last ever concert with it.

1977 was a landmark year for Kiss. They had released two top ten albums, while *Alive!*, *Destroyer*, and *Rock and Roll Over* all lingered in the top 200. On two separate occasions that year, Kiss had four albums in the *Billboard* chart at the same time. Additionally, their first three albums had been repackaged and released as *The Originals*, which charted for a month prior to *Love Gun* being issued. They remained one of the biggest live draws in the United States and were phenomenally successful in Japan, where their four sold-out shows at the Budokan equalled a record previously set by the Beatles. They had scored a People's Choice Award and were America's favourite band according to Gallup. On top of this, they dominated the front covers of the music and teen press and had a Marvel comic that sold half a million copies.

But 1977 is also now recognised as marking the end of an era, the passing of the Golden Age of Kiss. Frehley, having finally found his voice, wanted to go solo. Criss, having co-written the band's biggest hit, also wanted to go solo. The other three resented that it was predominantly Simmons that appeared on magazine covers. Criss was a coke fiend, and Frehley an alcoholic. Paul was playing bass and lead guitar on his songs; Ace was doing the same on his. No one knew it at the time, but *Love Gun* was the last album the quartet would work on as a cohesive unit.

'We weren't speaking to each other,' wrote Stanley in *Face the Music*. 'We couldn't stand each other.' The illusion of Kiss would be maintained for a few more years, but it was all smoke and mirrors, and the mirrors were cracked.

1978: Kiss Meets the Phantom of the Park and the Solo Albums

Kiss!
That's the name.
Kiss!
They may look insane.
Kiss!
If rock's your game,
It's Kiss!

This was the inane advertising jingle that accompanied an advert for the latest addition to the never-ending Kiss merchandise onslaught, four Kiss dolls released by Mego in 1978. The figures came dressed in the Love Gun costumes, and with cardboard cut-out instruments. Mego wanted to use the same facial mould for all the faces, but Rock Steady stood their ground and insisted on individual likenesses. Despite this, the head for the Paul Stanley figure was recycled from a previous doll of Daryl Dragon AKA the Captain from the poor-selling Captain & Tennille line. 'You can put them in any crazy pose you want,' advises the voiceover, as four young teenagers (two boys, two girls, one of whom is black – they were really going for that all-inclusive demography) do precisely that. No doubt poor old 'Tennille' found herself in some 'crazy poses' with 'Gene Simmons', at least when Gene Simmons was playing with them.

Apart from the internal frictions, Kiss were now a band without a clear identity. They sang incessantly about sex, but their faces were being slapped on a bewildering range of products aimed primarily at children. This process had begun inadvertently with the band members portrayed as fantasy characters on the *Destroyer* cover and continued with the issuing of the *Kiss* comic book. Now there were the Kiss dolls, Kiss bubble gum cards, a 'Kiss on Tour' board game, toy guitars, and a Kiss phonograph, a red and white plastic turntable adorned with the cover shots from *Alive II* on which only 7-inch singles could be played. The audience at a Kiss concert were now considerably younger than the one captured in Fin Costello's *Alive!* back cover photograph.

In their respective memoirs, band members react to this shift from band to brand. Frehley: 'At the same time we were trying to branch out with an album like *Destroyer*, we were aggressively peddling merchandise to ten-year-old kids. I remember feeling that we were getting too commercialised for our own good, and that some of the toys probably turned off the serious rockers who might have been our fans'. Criss's assessment of the situation was devastatingly succinct: 'I didn't want to do this anymore. We had become a fucking Barbie doll-selling lowlife piece-of-shit merchandise band'.

And it was about to get worse. The Golden Age may have been over, but Bill Aucoin was about to launch the next era of the band. In his revealing book *Kiss and Sell: the Making of a Supergroup*, Chris Lendt coined the perfect name for it: Super Kiss.

The idea had a simple foundation: Kiss was now too big a band to be running on the annual album-tour-album-tour hamster wheel. It was time to evolve from rock superstars into pop culture icons. The *Love Gun* tour, which had morphed into the *Alive II* tour, would end stateside in early February, and at the end of March, the band would be back in Japan for three dates at the Budokan. After that, they would be off the road after four years of solid touring. For the remainder of the year, the band would be focusing on two new projects that would begin their transformation into Super Kiss.

Because of the time required to work on these new endeavours, Aucoin and Bogart were concerned about the lack of new Kiss product, so they decided on a stopgap in the shape of the band's first greatest hits package *Double Platinum*. The band's only involvement was to re-record 'Strutter' at Bogart's request, who, according to Stanley, wanted the new version to have 'more of a quote unquote disco feel'. The result, 'Strutter '78', didn't sound that far removed from the original, but it did allow Kiss to collaborate with producer Jimmy Ienner, who had overseen all the Raspberries' records. This 'new' track was also a blatant attempt to hook fans that already had all the albums. The rest of the tracks were remixed by Sean Delaney and Mike Stone, mainly to prevent the earlier tinny tracks and even the crisp Kramer cuts from jarring with Bob Ezrin's bombast on the *Destroyer* songs. Despite its title, *Double Platinum* sold a 'mere' million copies, so should more accurately be called *Single Platinum*. Or just *Platinum*.

The first of the Super Kiss projects was an exercise in sheer ego and audacity, comprising as it did four solo albums, one from each member of the band. This wasn't uncommon – all four original members of the Who had released solo records by this time, for example – but no band had released a solo album from each band member *on the same day*. Apart from elevating Kiss to a new level, this idea had more pragmatic origins:

it was a strategy to prevent Kiss from splitting up. Ace Frehley and Peter Criss had both been making noises about leaving to start solo careers, but Aucoin persuaded them to remain, reasoning that, like the Who and others, they could both release their own albums and stay in the band (It should be noted that the solo albums weren't just some hurried together scheme to keep the band alive; they were part of the deal when Kiss renegotiated with Casablanca in 1976 and signed into reality in January 1977. This just reinforces how long the rot had set in).

There was nothing in those contracts regarding the albums being released simultaneously, however, and Casablanca were far from thrilled with this idea. Here's Larry Harris in *And Party Every Day: The Inside Story of Casablanca Records*:

> We hated the idea and did our best to stonewall Aucoin. Solo albums were a lose-lose proposition for a record company. They rarely did well, so financially, they made little sense, but by saying no to your artists, you ran the risk of fracturing the always-fragile act-label relationship. Kiss wanted to do four at once? No thanks.

Baulking at the thought of losing their grease painted cash cows, Casablanca relented. The simultaneous solo albums were greenlit and will be discussed later in this chapter.

The second project was a movie. This too was par for the course for rock acts in the 1970s: witness *Pink Floyd: Live at Pompeii* (1972), T. Rex's *Born to Boogie* (1972), Elvis Presley in *Aloha from Hawaii* (1973), Led Zeppelin's *The Song Remains the Same* (1976) Alice Cooper's *Welcome to My Nightmare* concert film (1976), to name but a few. However, the Kiss movie would be different; although it would contain some concert footage, the film would be a fantasy adventure with Kiss as superheroes, much as they were in the Marvel comic. It would be called *Kiss Meets the Phantom of the Park*.

According to Kiss, the movie was pitched to them as a cross between *A Hard Day's Night* and *Star Wars*. It was produced by Hanna-Barbera, creators of such iconic animated shows as *The Flintstones* and *Scooby Doo*, but relative newcomers to live action feature films, and was intended for television rather than theatre release. These two facts alone should have been enough to set alarm bells ringing, but alas, no. On the plus side, director Gordon Hessler had previous form, having directed a trio of Vincent Price vehicles (*The Oblong Box*, *Cry of the Banshee*, and *Scream and Scream Again* – this last-named starring a triumvirate of terror in the shape of Price, Christopher Lee, and Peter Cushing) and the box office hit *The Golden Voyage of Sinbad* (1974). He also had extensive experience working in American television, directing episodes of *Kolchak: The Night Stalker*, *Kung Fu*, and *Wonder Woman*, among others. Unfortunately, he seems to have brought none of his experience to bear on this movie, if indeed he was there for the entire shoot (see below).

Shooting took place throughout May, mostly at the Magic Mountain amusement park, with some interior filming done in Santa Clarita, and things did not go smoothly. Screenwriters Jan-Michael Sherman and Don Buday spent some time with Kiss to get a feel for their characters, but Frehley was in a non-communicative mood and would only respond by saying 'Awk!' or non-sequiturs like 'Thirteen for a dozen' or 'I kills 'em all'. Not unreasonably, Sherman and Buday decided Ace was an interplanetary Harpo Marx and wrote the awks into the script. When the guitarist saw this, he exploded at his lack of lines and seemed totally incapable of realising he himself had created the situation. Carefully crafted zingers like 'Insufficient data at this time, Starchild' were hastily scribbled for the Space Ace.

Predictably, Frehley and Criss's constant drinking and drugging meant that the 6 am wakeup calls went unappreciated, and neither possessed the patience to endure the waiting around associated with movie making. Here's Ace, recounting life on the movie set in *No Regrets*:

> A couple of times during the movie, I arrived bright and early, threw on my makeup and costume, and got all ready to go… and then sat in my trailer. After an hour or two, one of the assistant directors would stop by and say, 'You know what, Ace? We're doing some close-ups on Gene this morning, so I don't think we're going to need you until after lunch. Why don't you relax for a while?'
>
> That really made me crazy. Here I was, one of the 'stars' of the film, and you'd think maybe they could be a little more considerate? Maybe let me know the night before? Don't these fuckin' people plan?

Further adding to Peter Criss's lack of focus was the fact he had just met *Playboy* model Debra Jensen and had fallen head over heels in lust. As Criss, ever the silver-nosed charmer, so delicately puts it in *Makeup to Breakup*: 'Deb coming to the set spelt doom for the film. Who gave a shit about the movie anymore? I just wanted to get in her pants'.

Both he and Frehley would storm off the set at the drop of a hat, even during filming. On one now legendary occasion, in a scene involving a battle against robotic versions of Frankenstein's Monster and Dracula, an absent and huffing Frehley had been replaced by his stunt double, who was African American. Even the more disciplined Stanley and Simmons didn't bother learning lines (or indeed reading the script), preferring instead to just show up each day and having someone feed them their lines before filming. By Stanley's own admission, if they got through the line without flubbing it, it was a 'keeper'. How well it was acted never entered the equation. This scenario lends credence to Bill Aucoin's later assertion that Hessler was fired by Hanna-Barbera for devoting too much time in coaching Kiss in acting and was replaced by a jobsworth.

On 19 May, the band played their last show of the year, a one-off to allow concert scenes for the movie to be filmed. The audience was largely comprised of radio contest winners, and their invitations made it clear that this was not a regular Kiss concert: 'There will be breaks in between the songs as additional filming, equipment, and scenes are set. The foundations for special effects that will be added later in the film will be laid at this time.' Even during these show scenes, the band couldn't present a united front, as Stanley recalls in *Face the Music*: 'We had to play a fake concert at Magic Mountain amusement park for another scene. When we were onstage, I turned around and saw some random old man in cat makeup and a wig playing the drums and chewing gum. Peter had taken off, and they threw this guy up there'. Criss confirms this in *Makeup to Breakup*: 'I took my sticks and threw them into the drums and stormed off in my limo with Rosie (his bodyguard). They had to get some middle-aged stagehand to throw on one of my costumes and sit in my seat. They continued filming from different angles, so you couldn't really tell it wasn't me.'

A few pages earlier, Criss makes it clear where his mind was at. 'I sat there and figured that I had a lot of money now. I had a beautiful new girlfriend. I was about to do a solo album. What did I need this shit for? I was a big enough star that I could put together my own band and do well.' An emergency meeting was called, and Criss was persuaded to remain. If he finished the movie, he could then have a break from the others and work on his record, and everything would be okay. Though he stayed, he wasn't convinced Kiss had a future. 'It was really over by then. Even Gene and Paul knew it. They had had enough of mine and Ace's crap and we had certainly had enough of theirs. We weren't a band anymore.'

When filming concluded, the four members of the band went their separate ways to work on the solo albums. To add to Criss's woes, he promptly crashed his car after storming off the movie set and had to make his record with busted ribs and his fingers taped up to braces.

Still the merchandising machine pumped out the product. In August, the second Marvel *Kiss* comic limped onto the market with zero fanfare. There was no bloodletting at the printing presses, no photos with Stan Lee. By now, Steve Gerber was not only gone from Marvel but in dispute with them over ownership rights of his Howard the Duck character. Writing duties fell to assistant editor Ralph Macchio (*not* the Karate Kid actor), who was very much at the start of his career. That might not sound too promising for Kiss's further comic book capers, but Macchio's script was more coherent than Gerber's original, and he arguably does a better job of presenting the foursome's superhero personas. He even throws in a few Gerber-esque touches, not least when he has Kiss encounter that writer's homicidal Elf with a Gun, whose curiosity about the band curbs his usual murderous instincts. After aiding Kiss in their quest, he vanishes with the more characteristic promise, 'The next time we run into each other – I'll blow all your heads off'. Once the Elf has gone, the Starchild says, 'Nice guy. I hope he gets hit by a truck'. This is a neat in-joke on Macchio's part. The Elf had cropped up intermittently on Gerber's run on the *Defenders* comic book, killing random victims whenever he appeared. Gerber had left Marvel without ever concluding the Elf's story, and his replacement writer had no idea what to do with the character, so he wrote him out of the series by having him, yes, getting hit by a truck.

Macchio's dialogue sparkles in places, but his plot is strictly pedestrian. Once again empowered by the talismans of Khyscz, our heroes need to stop the villain of the piece, the Dark Lord, a generic bad guy with an equally generic name, from travelling through time, collecting 'the proper intensity of crowd-sustained emotional activity' which will somehow allow him to 'possess strength enough to trample the world beneath my feet.' Kiss battle the evildoer through time, at a '50s Rock 'n' Roll revue, at Woodstock, and at a '70s disco marathon, and naturally emerge triumphant. Incredibly, this is a far better plot than *Kiss Meets the Phantom of the Park*, but, as we shall see later, that ain't saying much.

The art is also better than on the band's first comic book outing, not least because it is drawn by one artist rather than the many hands involved in the original. Again, it is by a relative newcomer, John Romita Jr., but he would go on to become one of the industry's top talents and would, like his father, enjoy a celebrated run on Marvel's flagship title, *The Amazing Spider-Man*.

The solo albums dropped on 18 September, housed behind classy portraits painted by Eraldo Carugati. Casablanca Record's art director Dennis Woloch was again charged with designing the sleeves, and he elected against full figure shots or character-reflective environments in favour of close-ups. As he told Claudio Bergamin in their excellent series of YouTube interviews, he wanted the images to have a 'timeless' quality. Woloch hired Carugeti – who only had one album cover to his name, Rush's *Fly by Night* – and gave him the 1977-1978 Kiss concert program as reference, and all the cover portraits bar Frehley's are based on the photographs on the front cover of that tour book (Note: those same photographs were earlier used for the embossed foil portraits that grace the inner gatefold of *Double Platinum*).

It was Woloch that also decided on the colours that represented each member of the band. Carugati's original paintings had them all backlit by the same-coloured light, and although Woloch liked this effect, he thought each of them having a different coloured 'aura' would enable each album to stand out in record store displays and racks. He picked red, representing blood and fire, for Simmons; Ace ideally would have got black to represent outer space, but that would not have worked aesthetically, so he got blue for the sky; and Criss's green represents the jungle through which he, as a big cat, stalks. Woloch admits being stumped when it came to Stanley – what exactly *was* a Starchild? – but settled on purple when he was reminded that Stanley's character had previously being designated the Lover, and purple was the colour of passion (an error on Woloch's part, as red is usually associated with love). So as not to distract from Carugati's art, Woloch opted to make the Kiss logo at the top left corner of the cover and the artist's name at the top right transparent; he later said he wished he had left them off the front altogether.

Woloch also commissioned David Edward Byrd to illustrate the posters that came with each album. Byrd had designed many fine posters for Broadway shows (*Godspell*, *Little Shop of Horrors*) and concerts at the Filmore East (Pink Floyd, Rolling Stones, Jefferson Airplane), many of which showed a strong Art Nouveau influence; closer to home, he was also responsible for the Casablanca Records logo. Unfortunately, the Kiss posters don't represent his best work as he was given a tight deadline, resulting in the finished art looking flat and cartoony and displaying none of the depth, detail, or warmth that usually characterises his work. This being Kiss, each poster also served as part of a four-piece jigsaw puzzle, a blatant ploy to encourage fans to purchase all four albums. As a further inducement, anyone buying the four got to take them home in a special record shop plastic bag adorned with all the album covers; they now sell on eBay for about forty bucks.

One cover addition that wasn't down to Woloch was the mawkish back cover dedications, where each band member dedicated their album to the other three. This presumably originated with Aucoin and was a desperate attempt to perpetuate an illusion of unity about the band, but it comes across as both insincere and schmaltzy with a capital 'S'. Criss deviates from the party line slightly by adding his old Chelsea and Lips bandmate Michael Benvenga to his dedication; Benvenga had passed away the previous year, aged 28.

Peter Criss

Personnel:
Peter Criss: lead vocals, backing vocals, drums on all tracks except 6, 7, and 10, percussion on track 8
Alan Schwartzberg: drums on tracks 6, 7, and 10
Bill Bodine: bass guitar on tracks 1-5 and 9
Neil Jason: bass guitar on tracks 6, 7, and 10
Art Munson: guitars on tracks 1- 5 and 9
Stan Penridge: guitars on 1-5 and 8- 9, backing vocals
Elliot Randell: guitars on 'Easy Thing' and 'I Can't Stop the Rain'
John Tropea: guitars on tracks 6, 7, and 10
Brendan Harkin: guitars on 'Easy Thing'
Steve Lukather: guitar solo on 'That's the Kind of Sugar Papa Likes' and 'Hooked on Rock and Roll'
Bill Cuomo: keyboards on tracks 1- 5 and 9
Richard Gerstein: keyboard on tracks 6, 7, and 10
Davey Faragher, Tommy Faragher, Danny Faragher, Jimmy Faragher, Maxine Dixon, Maxine Willard, Julia Tillman, Annie Sutton, Gordon Grody: backing vocals
Tom Saviano: horn arrangements
Michael Carnahan: saxophone solo on 'Tossin' and Turnin'', baritone sax on 'Hooked on Rock and Roll'
Recorded at Electric Lady Studios, New York City, Burbank Studios, Burbank, California, and Sunset Sound, Hollywood, California, April-July 1978
Produced by: Vini Poncia

Released: 18 September 1978
Running time: 34.39
Highest chart place: US: 43
Tracklisting: 1. 'I'm Gonna Love You' (Criss, Penridge) 3.18, 2. 'You Matter to Me' (Poncia, Vastano, Morgan) 3.15, 3. 'Tossin' and Turnin'' (Adams, Rene) 3.58, 4. 'Don't You Let Me Down' (Criss, Penridge) 3.38, 5. 'That's the Kind of Sugar Papa Likes' (Criss, Penridge) 2.59, 6. 'Easy Thing' (Criss Penridge) 3.53, 7. 'Rock Me, Baby' (Delaney) 2.50, 8. 'Kiss the Girl Goodbye' (Criss, Penridge) 2.46, 9. 'Hooked on Rock 'n' Roll (Criss, Penridge) 3.37, 10. 'I Can't Stop the rain' (Delaney) 4.25

Album opener 'I'm Gonna Love You' is by Criss and his frequent collaborator Stan Penridge, and, like 'Beth' and 'Baby Driver', is a song that dates to Criss's Lips days. There are another three such songs on *Peter Criss*, not to mention a cover and two tracks penned by Sean Delaney, all of which suggest the Catman did not have songwriting chops (A quick scan of his later solo albums all but confirm this. Criss has at least one songwriting partner on every track that bears his name, while 1982's *Let Me Rock You* is essentially a covers album bar one song). Being neither experienced nor prolific in this area did not bode well for his album. On the plus side, Criss's solo effort was arguably the most experimental of the four solo albums, as he throws away Kiss's pop-metal template in favour of blue-eyed soul and R&B.

Criss immediately sets out his stall with 'I'm Gonna Love You', a mid-tempo slice of funk complete with horns and female backing singers. The midnight cat-fight screech that he utilised on such Kiss tracks as 'Black Diamond' and 'Baby Driver' is abandoned, and the drummer's smoke and whisky vocal coupled with the exuberance of the other performers make for a strong opening track.

Unfortunately, the album takes an early dip with 'You Matter to Me', a lacklustre disco-lite track written by producer Vini Poncia, in conjunction with Michael Morgan and John Vastano (whose band White Water, also produced by Poncia, had recorded material not dissimilar to that on the *Peter Criss* album). This was the second single from the album, but despite being released at the height of disco fever, it filled no floors and troubled no charts. In 1978, Poncia was most associated with another drummer, Ringo Starr, having co-written and played on *Ringo* (1973), *Goodnight Vienna* (1974), and *Ringo the 4th* (1977). He also cowrote songs on *Ringo's Rotogravure* (1976) and produced Starr's *Bad Boy* album mere months before commencing work on Criss's platter. The previous year he had also co-written Leo Sayer's chart-topping, Grammy-winning 'You Make Me Feel Like Dancing'. Despite this track record, Poncia was not Criss's first choice, with Jimmy Iovine, Tom Dowd, and Giorgio Moroder all being considered.

Things don't improve any with 'Tossin' and Turnin'', a straight if slightly slower reading of the Bobby Lewis 1961 original. Criss's primary motivation for recording it was that he could relate to it, being an insomniac. Kiss played the song, without ever looking entirely comfortable, on early dates of 1979's *Dynasty* tour.

'Don't You Let Me Down', another Criss/Penridge original from the Lips vault, partially lifts the album up again. Poncia gives it a lush Ben E. King-era Drifters makeover, which, thanks to Criss's soulful lead, effective R&B vocal group backing from the Catman, Penridge, and Poncia, sparse drumming, and an evocative Brill Building bassline from Bill Bodine, is entirely convincing. *Peter Criss* was the only solo album to spawn two singles, and this was the first. It was unsuccessful.

So far, Criss has been all sweet and soulful, but there is a Kiss logo on the album cover, so the kids want some songs about sex, goddammit! Well, they're in luck because here's 'That's the Kind of Sugar Papa Likes', a song that so wants to be 'Swing Your Daddy' when it grows up. Yet another Lips leftover, the most interesting thing about this is the title, taken from a line spoken by Humphrey Bogart's character Fred C. Dobbs in the 1948 film *The Treasure of Sierra Madre*.

'Easy Thing' is a Criss/Penridge collaboration actually written for this album rather than a previous band. It is an acoustic, softer-than-soft number that eventually morphs into a power ballad and features what is possibly Criss's best vocal performance. It's a top tune with clear commercial appeal, one of those songs that seems destined to be covered many times yet never was. Of some amusement is a story told to Tim McPhate by guitarist Brendan Harkin, of Bill Aucoin's 'other' group Starz, and published in Julian Gill's *Gene, Ace, Peter, & Paul: A Detailed Exploration of the 1978 Kiss Solo Albums*. In essence, Harkin, who recalls playing on several tracks on *Peter Criss*, was pulled to the side by Sean Delaney and told he would only be credited for his playing on 'Easy Thing'. The reason given was that Criss didn't want to credit 'people who are not huge stars'. If true, it is a statement commensurate with both Criss's cocaine-fuelled-I-won-a-People's-Award ego at the time (and, once again, congratulations on tying with 'Disco Duck', sir), and his detachment from reality. The Catman's record was populated with topflight musicians, such as Allan Schwartzberg, who had drummed on Harry Chapin's 'Cat's in the Cradle', Gloria Gaynor's 'Never Can Say Goodbye', and Peter Gabriel's 'Solsbury Hill', amongst many others, but the 'huge stars' Criss referred to were all over at the Manor in Oxfordshire working on Gene Simmons' album.

Every so often, an interview will crop up with a well-known musician in which they will reminisce how one of their much-beloved and biggest-selling songs was in fact, written on the back of a cocktail napkin. Sean Delaney's 'Rock Me, Baby' sounds like one of those songs, but without the love or the sales.

'Maybe I'll write another 'Beth'', was a statement Criss was prone to say in interviews at the time. Sadly, with 'Kiss the Girl Goodbye', he and Penridge attempt precisely that, conjuring up one of those rare songs that, upon hearing, compels the listener to have a shower. And nothing in Criss's (admittedly limited) back catalogue prepares said listener for that dog-startling falsetto. Unlike 'Beth', which Criss had originally claimed was about his wife, 'Kiss the Girl Goodbye' really is about Lydia and the disintegration of their marriage. Lydia, who had worked her proverbial socks off to allow Peter to 'follow his dreams', i.e., not work, deserved a better kiss-off than this half-baked schmaltz. This is by far the worst song on the album, a remarkable statement considering it also contains 'That's the Kind of Sugar Papa Likes' and 'Rock Me, Baby'.

'Hooked on Rock 'n' Roll' is the fourth and final number plundered from the Criss-Penridge past, and despite its title, it sounds as if Mr. Criss is more accurately hooked on some bar room blues and a little bit of boogie-woogie.

The album ends with another Sean Delaney song, the grandiose ballad 'I Can't Stop the Rain'. It starts sparsely, as grandiose ballads are wont to do, with melancholy piano, here played by Richard Gerstein (who would later adopt the stage name Richard T. Bear). The other musicians enter in stages, a restrained Neil Jason (bass) and Allan Schwartzberg (drums) making their presence felt when Criss starts singing, and guitarists John Tropea and Elliott Randall coming in on the chorus, as does the string section arranged by Bill Cuomo. This gradual instrumental build-up when it comes to balladry may be an overused technique, but that doesn't negate its effectiveness one iota, and 'I Can't Stop the Rain' is far superior to Delaney's earlier contribution.

This song contains the line 'Then a cold wind came calling / Strange how it knew me by my name', which must surely be the best couplet to ever appear under the Kiss banner. How disappointing then to check the lyrics while preparing this book, only to discover it is actually 'Then a cold wind came calling / Strange how it knew it'd bother me,' and that I had been mishearing it for decades. Spare him his life from his pork sausages and all that.

Some of the above players – Gerstein, Jason, Schwartzberg, and Randall – pulled double-duty and appeared on Gene Simmons' album.

Peter Criss was the least successful of the four, reaching number 43 on the *Billboard* chart. In a failed attempt to bolster sales, Casablanca released two singles from the album, but neither charted. The critics weren't any kinder than the consumer. Robert Duncan of *Rolling Stone* said the album 'couldn't be worse', while Joel McNally of *Summit Press* said the album 'had one song, 'I Can't Stop the Rain', which could even be on a grown-up album one day.' Even *Sounds'* resident Kiss superfan Geoff Barton concluded that 'the most complimentary word I can find for the LP is pleasant'.

Most scathing were Criss's bandmates Stanley and Simmons. Asked to rate Criss's album for *Behind the Mask*, published in 2003, Stanley says, 'That album I just don't get. I can't give it any stars'. Simmons was equally dismissive: 'Zero. Out of all the records we have ever done solo or as a group, I think that one showed that the guy behind it didn't really have a clue'.

Ace Frehley

Personnel:
Ace Frehley: lead vocals, backing vocals, lead guitar, rhythm guitar, acoustic guitar, guitar synthesiser, bass guitar
Anton Fig: drums, percussion
Will Lee: bass guitar on 'Ozone', 'I'm in Need of Love', and 'Wiped-Out'
Carl Tallarico: drums on 'Fractured Mirror'
David Lasley and Susan Collins: backing vocals on 'Speedin' Back to My Baby', 'What's On Your Mind?', and 'New York Groove'
Larry Kelly: backing vocals on 'Rip It Out'
Bill 'Bear' Scheniman: bell on 'Fractured Mirror'
Bobby McAdams: talkbox on 'New York Groove'
Recorded at The Mansion, Sharon, Connecticut, and Plaza Sound Studios, New York City, June-July 1978
Produced by Eddie Kramer and Ace Frehley
Released: 18 September 1978

Running time: 36.44
Highest chart place: US: 26
Tracklisting: 1. 'Rip It Out' (Frehley, L. Kelly, S. Kelly) 3.40, 2. 'Speedin' Back to My Baby' (Frehley, J. Frehley) 3.37, 3. 'Snow Blind' (Frehley) 3.55, 4. 'Ozone' (Frehley) 4.43, 'What's On Your Mind?' (Frehley) 3.28, 6. 'New York Groove' (Ballard) 3.03, 7. 'I'm in Need of Love' (Frehley) 4.39, 8. 'Wiped-Out' (Frehley, Fig) 4.13, 9. 'Fractured Mirror' (Frehley) 5.26

Ace Frehley's solo outing thunders into life with the raw and raucous 'Rip It Out'. It is a hard rocking classic that sets out Ace's stall as plainly as 'I'm Going to Love You' did Peter's. The difference is that Frehley maintains the quality throughout. 'Rip It Out' is essentially the work of a power trio, with Frehley playing both the guitarist and bassist roles, and Anton Fig providing the drumming. This song, with its double-tracked drum solo, and album, served as the world's introduction to Fig, who, because of his South African origins, was soon nicknamed 'the Thunder from Down Under'. He would go on to have a hugely successful career as both a session musician and, from 1986, as the drummer in the World's Most Dangerous Band (later the CBS Orchestra), the house band on *Late Night with David Letterman*. He would also become a member of Frehley's post-Kiss band, Frehley's Comet, and would play on some of the guitarist's twenty-first-century albums. He would also have a role to play in the next two Kiss albums, as we shall see in later chapters.

Frehley co-wrote 'Rip It Out' with Larry Kelly, who had been the lead vocalist in Cathedral and Magic People, two of the guitarist's earlier bands. Kelly also provided backing vocals on this track, and Kelly's wife Sue was also listed as one of the song's co-writers.

'Speedin' Back to My Baby' is a fun little choogle that suggests what Creedence Clearwater Revival might have sounded like if they had been born in the Bronx rather than the bayou. It is arguably one of the poppiest, most fun songs in the entire Kiss catalogue, and it bops along so merrily we will forgive it that clichéd chorus couplet of 'Speedin' back to my baby / And I don't mean maybe'. This is the only collaboration between Frehley and his wife Jeanette, but, based on this evidence, they really should have written together more.

A quick word about the backing vocalists David Lasley and Susan Collins, who also appear on 'What's on Your Mind' and 'New York Groove'. Lasley was a successful songwriter, with Dionne Warwick, Whitney Houston, Bonnie Raitt, and Chaka Khan amongst the many who recorded his material. He also recorded and toured as a backing singer for many artists, most notably with James Taylor. In 1982, he reached 32 on the *Billboard* Hot 100 as a solo artist, with 'If I had My Wish Tonight'. Despite his pedigree, he is outperformed here by Collins, who gives the fade out of 'Speedin' Back to My Baby' a soulful flourish. She had previously worked with Jimi Hendrix, Brian Wilson, and Todd Rundgren, and would later tour with the Electric Light Orchestra.

'Snow Blind' is all doom-laden Sabbath riffing, and a neat bit of scheduling given the lightness of the previous track. Write about what you know, runs the adage, so Ace describes his by then frequent states of cocaine catalepsy. 'Ozone' is another unsubtle narcotics canticle ('I'm the kind of guy / Who likes getting high') that would never have made it onto a regular Kiss record. However, the lyrics are strictly functional, even by Kiss standards, as 'Ozone' is more of a musical workout than a song, with some acoustic guitar adding warmth to the hard rocking, and Frehley is clearly enjoying the creative freedom away from the constraints of the band. This is the first of three tracks in which Anton Fig is joined by future CBS Orchestra bandmate, bass player Will Lee.

'What's On Your Mind' maintains the heavy riffing, and again features some prominent acoustic playing, this time on a twelve-string, but Frehley maintains the album's freshness by wandering into power pop territory and his soloing behind the final chorus is simple and exquisite. With lines like 'I can't express the words to tell you / 'Bout the feelings I've got locked up inside', Frehley also stumbles dangerously close to vulnerability, something strictly prohibited in the Kiss rulebook. Fortunately, he gets back on track by blowing it with the next line, 'If only you would give me a reason / Why you're so uptight,' a sentence destined to end more conversations than it starts. Collins and Lasley are back on backing vocal duties and enhance the song's pop sensibilities.

Side two opens with the only cover version on the album, Russ Ballard's classic 'New York Groove'. The 'I'm back in the New York Groove' phrase occurred to Ballard when he was flying there to master Roger Daltrey's *Ride a Rock Horse* album in early 1975, and he finished writing the song in the studio when he was recording it with British glam-poppers Hello. Their version reached number nine in the UK charts.

In his autobiography, Frehley recalls that it was one of producer Eddie Kramer's assistants that suggested the song for the album, and that he (Frehley) 'frankly didn't think that much of it the first time I heard it'. However, Kramer pushed for its inclusion, thinking it a perfect vehicle for

Frehley. The guitarist remained unconvinced, but he acquiesced because he trusted Kramer's judgement.

The Bo Diddley acka-acka rhythm throughout the song was produced using a talkbox like the device Peter Frampton popularised on *Frampton Comes Alive!* Frehley did the guitar playing but couldn't work out how to simultaneously use the mouthpiece, so his friend Bobby McAdams fulfilled that duty. 'New York Groove' marks the final appearance on *Ace Frehley* of Lasley and Collins, with Collins' vocals being triple-tracked.

'New York Groove' reached thirteen on the *Billboard* chart when released as a single and was the most successful single from the four solo albums. Not surprisingly, Frehley has since warmed to the song: 'It's a great song for a guy from the Bronx, which is what I still am after all these years. It was a total departure from both Kiss and my personal style and taste, but it was absolutely the right song at the right time'. And what did Ballard think of Frehley's take on his song? 'He did a great version. There was a little bit more attitude because Hello were kind of young and I think they sounded young… I was just throwing it out to them, and they were sort of copying what I was doing initially. When Ace did his thing on it, it sounded a bit more mature. He brought a hooligan, tough guy kind of attitude to it'.

'New York Groove' was far from the only Kiss / Ballard connection. Kiss had supported Argent, of whom Ballard was then a member, on a few dates in 1974, Ace revisited the Ballard songbook on the *Frehley's Comet* album ('Into the Night'), Criss covered the Ballard-penned 'Some Kinda Hurricane' and 'Let Me Rock You' on *Let Me Rock You* (1982), and Kiss covered Argent's 'God Gave Rock and Roll to You' in 1991.

The use of echoes and delays gives 'I'm in Need of Love' an otherworldly texture, making it the track most appropriate for Frehley's Space Ace persona (the 'Spaceman' name had yet to be coined). Like the earlier 'Snow Blind', this song features a double-time guitar solo.

'Wiped-Out' acknowledges its near namesake, the Surfaris' 'Wipe Out', by opening with a drum solo / echo-drenched manic laughter combo like that heard on the 1963 hit. It remains heavily percussive throughout, which might be down to 'Wiped-Out' being a co-write with Anton Fig. To his credit, Frehley has stayed clear of Kiss's usual 'You Wanna Have Sex with Me' lyrical riff, but that might just be because he was incapable of getting it up due to the substance abuse that is a recurring theme of this album. Unlike the coke of 'Snow Blind' and 'Ozone', it is the demon drink that is being serenaded now, as snatches such as 'I was blind as a skunk' and 'I took your hand and tried to stand and ended up sitting back down' make clear, but the effect is pretty much the same; Ace was wiped out and had his lights out. Yep.

The album ends with 'Fractured Mirror', the first instrumental to appear on a Kiss-related album since 'Love Theme from Kiss' on the band's debut, although the current number is more epic than that earlier track. It opens with the sound of a pealing bell, over which an acoustic ostinato fades in, and then another, the song becoming a series of ever-joining layers, building up until a bass, a couple of electric guitars, and a guitar synthesiser join the acoustics in the mix. This is the sole track on which Anton Fig does not appear, but replacement Carl Tallarico foregoes the thunder to keep things simple, his beat the bedrock upon which the other instrumentation is built. And then, when the piece has reached cacophonous proportions, it all falls away, leaving just the drum beat and the acoustic guitars.

It is the closest Frehley would ever get to prog or, more appropriately in his case, space rock; the tune is structurally similar to Hawkwind's 'Wind of Change' track from three years earlier. The guitarist clearly enjoyed the experiment, as he subsequently closed all his Frehley's Comet and solo records (bar the *Origins* covers albums) with an instrumental, often with a name, such as 'Fractured Too' or 'Fractured Quantum', that reflected 'Fractured Mirror's title.

Ace Frehley was the bestselling album of the four, spending 23 weeks on the *Billboard* chart and peaking at 26. In 'New York Groove', it was also the only one to produce a bona-fide hit single. Frehley's album was also a hit with the press. Billy Altman of *The Village Voice* thought Ace's record exuded 'all the sledgehammer, turn-me-loose madness of great metalloid hard rock' before concluding that 'there's an unassuming, unpretentious force at work here that puts the other Kiss boys to shame'. When discussing Paul Stanley's album, Geoff Barton of *Sounds* said it 'would probably be the best of the bunch if not for the remarkable efforts of Ace', and then awarded the axeman's platter the full five stars.

Considering he had only contributed a half dozen solo songs the Kiss canon to date, Stanley and Simmons probably didn't expect much from Frehley, so they must have been left slack-jawed when they heard his album and tracked its success. Yet they only gave it 'close to three' and three stars respectively in *Behind the Mask*, although, as with Peter Criss's effort, their scoring seems based on the person rather than the album. Really, guys, you need to get over it, whatever exactly 'it' is.

Gene Simmons

Personnel:
Gene Simmons: vocals, guitars, acoustic guitar
Neil Jason: bass
Elliot Randall: guitars
Allan Schwartzberg: drums
Sean Delaney: percussion, backing vocals
Eric Troyer: piano and vocals on 'Radioactive' and 'Living in Sin'
Steve Lacey: guitars on 'Radioactive'
John Shane Howell: classical guitar, segue between 'Radioactive' and 'Burning Up with Fever'
Richard Gerstein: piano on 'True Confessions' and 'Always Near You / Nowhere to Hide'
Joe Perry: guitars on 'Radioactive' and 'Tunnel of Love'
Bob Seger: backing vocals on 'Radioactive' and 'Tunnel of Love'
Rick Neilsen: guitars on 'See You in Your Dreams'
Helen Reddy: backing vocals on 'True Confessions'
Jeff 'Skunk' Baxter: guitars on 'Burning Up with Fever', 'See You Tonite', 'Tunnel of Love', and 'Mr. Make Believe'
Donna Summer: backing vocals on 'Burning Up with Fever' and 'Tunnel of Love'
Janis Ian: backing vocals on the 'Prelude to Radioactive'
Cher: spoken word phone call on 'Living in Sin'
Michael Des Barres: backing vocals on 'See You in Your Dreams'
Richie Ranno: guitars on 'Tunnel of Love'
Gordon Grody, Diva Gray, Kate Segal, Franny Eisenberg, Carolyn Ray: backing vocals
The Citrus College Singers: chorus on 'True Confessions' and 'Always Near You / Nowhere to Hide'
Ron Frangipane: symphonic arrangements and conductor of Members of the New York and Los Angeles Philharmonic Orchestras
Recorded at The Manor, Oxfordhire, Cherokee Studios, Los Angeles, and Blue Rock Studio, New York City, April-July 1978
Produced by: Gene Simmons and Sean Delaney
Released: 18 September 1978
Running time: 38.58
Highest chart place: US: 22
Tracklisting: 1. 'Radioactive' (Simmons) 3.50, 2. 'Burning Up with Fever' (Simmons) 4.19, 3. 'See You Tonite' (Simmons) 2.30, 4. 'Tunnel of Love' (Simmons) 3.49, 5. 'True Confessions' (Simmons) 3.30, 'Living in Sin' (Simmons, Delaney, Marks) 3.50,

7. 'Always Near You / Nowhere to Hide' (Simmons) 4.12, 8. 'Man of 1,000 Faces' (Simmons) 3.16, 9. 'Mr. Make Believe' (Simmons) 4.00, 10. 'SeeYou in Your Dreams' (Simmons) 2.48, 11. 'When You Wish Upon a Star' (Washington, Harline) 2.44

From the album that had the fewest number of performers (9) to the one with the greatest (24, plus the Citrus College Singers *and* Members of the New York and Los Angeles Philharmonic Orchestras), here is the ego-fest that is *Gene Simmons*, with guest stars galore.

The prelude that opens 'Radioactive' is suitably grandiose, all discordant, pseudo-classical strings and found sounds written and arranged by Ron Frangipane. Sean Delaney shouts 'Sanctum!' every so often, and Janis Ian sings semi-Gregorian chants, apparently in Latin. Delaney is playing the devil and Ian portrays a nun, but what any of this has to do with anything is never explained. The strings rise to a frantic conclusion, and then 'Radioactive' truly begins, somewhat underwhelming after that grand introduction. Apparently written for Jerry Lee Lewis until Bill Aucoin said nay, the song is essentially a Fifties rocker refracted through a Kiss prism; it could comfortably have sat on *Love Gun*.

Bob Seger provides backing vocals and Joe Perry slings the six-string, but, as with Janis Ian, one wonders why they bothered. They are unidentifiable, completely buried in the mix, and Perry doesn't even do the guitar solo (that honour going to Steve Lacey). Their appearance here seems primarily about enabling Simmons' sense of self.

An edited version was released as a single and reached 47 on the *Billboard* chart. Surprisingly, it fell just one place short of breaching the UK top forty, making 'Radioactive' the most successful Kiss or Kiss-related single in that country in the 1970s. It was also played on the mothership's *Dynasty* tour in 1979.

A raucous 'one-two, one-two-three-four', introduces 'Burning Up with Fever', but then segues to some classical guitar rather than the expected rawk and roll. It's a neat touch of misdirection, but it only temporarily holds the rocker at bay. 'Burning Up with Fever' is standard Simmons fare, originally demoed for *Destroyer* but rejected by Bob Ezrin, but the rhythm section adds a touch of funk, and at least this time, the guest stars, in this case, Donna Summer and Jeff 'Skunk' Baxter, can be clearly heard.

For track three, Simmons returns to the '60s and his Bullfrog Bheer songbook to resurrect an absolute corker. 'See You Tonite' is not without faults, the lack of a discernible chorus and lyrics that repeat the same four lines suggesting the song might not even have reached completion, but what is presented here is so strong it successfully stands as is. An acoustic ballad with swelling strings in the closing third, this song is a contender for being the most Beatle-y song not written by a Beatle, as well as being possibly Simmons' best song period. It is *that* good, and it came as no surprise when Kiss revived it for their appearance on *MTV Unplugged*.

Sadly, the sweetness doesn't last long because next up is 'Tunnel of Love', which features such 'sensitive' lyrics as 'You wanted my disease, you'll have to do as I please'. Oh dear. Far more interesting than the song is its background. The Van Halen brothers played on the original demo of this *Love Gun* reject, and Simmons apparently initially considered Ace Frehley for the guitar solo. Presumably, this proved a logistical impossibility with Frehley recording his own album, so Richie Ranno of Starz stepped in instead.

'True Confessions', also demoed for *Destroyer*, starts as a typical Gene song but takes a surprising but enjoyable left turn when it hits the chorus, which is all rock and roll piano and gospel vocals. Amongst the backing vocalists is Helen Reddy, a huge hitmaker in 1970s America with three number ones to her name. She was also considered a feminist icon and is, therefore, probably the last person one would expect on a Kiss record. Frehley wasn't impressed with Simmons' different guest star per song approach, and doesn't mince his words in *No Regrets*:

> I was dumbfounded sometimes by the stuff that would come out of Gene's mouth. He didn't know the difference between what was cool and what wasn't cool. I mean, come on. How could you not know that Helen Reddy (nothing personal, mind you), in 1978, was a very bad idea?

'True Confessions' also features a brief chorale by the Citrus College Singers, but Frehley's thoughts on that have gone unrecorded.

'Living in Sin' is the only original song on the album not solely penned by Simmons. The ever-dependable Sean Delaney gets a co-credit, as does, bizarrely, Howard Marks, one of Kiss's business managers, who contributed the 'Living in Sin at the Holiday Inn' line. At first glance, it too could be dismissed as typical Simmons, but the spoken word intro, heavy breathing, offbeat vocal delivery, the 'Hello, baby' nod to the Big Bopper, and Cher's turn as a hysterical groupie all suggest this song has a sense of humour, so would have been unlikely to have made it onto a Kiss album.

Simmons had reputedly approached all the former Beatles about guesting on the album, but for one reason or another, it never happened.

He opted instead to hire Mitch Weissman and Joe Pecorino, who were then playing McCartney and Lennon respectively in the successful Broadway musical revue *Beatlemania*, to provide backing vocals on 'Always Near You / Nowhere to Hide'. This, of course, is identical to not having the Beatles on your record, and Weissman and Pecorino don't even bring their fabbest voices to the table (although they also appeared on 'See You Tonite', where they were more successful in nailing that Beatles sound).

Despite this, 'Always Near You / Nowhere to Hide' still strongly invokes McCartney and co., circa *Revolver* and *The White Album*, and is the closest Simmons would ever get to psychedelia. The Fabs' influence is also there insofar as the bassist created this song by grafting two unfinished pieces together, *a la* 'A Day in the Life' or the *Abbey Road* medley. 'Always Near You' is structured layer by layer until it, and the listener, arrives at the 'Nowhere to Hide' section, wherein a returning Citrus College Choir accompany Simmons' most extraordinary vocal to deliver a thrilling, full-throated coda. It is the album's second classic after 'See You Tonite', and it remains Simmons' most adventurous piece.

Mitch Weissman would reappear in the Kiss story the following decade, co-writing three tracks for 1984's *Animalize* and one for *Crazy Nights* (1987).

Simmons remains musically adventurous on 'Man of 1,000 Faces', a tribute to one of his horror movie heroes, Lon Chaney, who was dubbed the Man of a Thousand Faces thanks to his incredible, self-taught makeup skills. He is best remembered for a couple of silent horror classics he made for Universal Studios, *The Hunchback of Notre Dame* (1923) and *The Phantom of the Opera* (1925).

This tune had been kicking around since the band's formation and had been mooted for inclusion on both *Dressed to Kill*, where it would have been hopelessly out of place, and *Destroyer*, where it would have felt at home, but Ezrin knocked it back. These delays probably worked in the song's favour, as Simmons was then able to take stock of ELO's phenomenal success in the latter half of the decade and follows their approach by marrying a Beatles-style melody to an orchestral arrangement. In a world where Casablanca were as adventurous as Simmons, this would have made for an excellent single choice. As an aside, Simmons originally planned to title his album after this track before the whole unified image-simultaneous release concept took hold.

'Mr. Make Believe' is another McCartney-esque, pre-Kiss soft rocker, another song pieced together from two unfinished demos, and another pop delight. It appears Gene Simmons is a better songwriter when he tries to be the Beatles' bassist rather than Kiss's.

'See You in Your Dreams' is a superfluous reworking of the *Rock and Roll Over* song, redone here as Simmons was reportedly unhappy with the original. Cheap Trick's Rick Nielsen provides lead guitar while backing vocals come courtesy of Michael Des Barres, who had headlined over Kiss as a member of Silverhead and supported them as part of Detective. Speaking of superfluous, the album closes with a cover of 'When You Wish Upon a Star', written for Walt Disney's 1940 adaptation of *Pinocchio*. This version sounds identical to the original, with Simmons' vocals substituted for that of Jiminy Cricket voice actor Cliff Edwards.

This aural horror aside, Simmons should be given credit for busting free from the Kiss confines for at least half these recordings. His songwriting is markedly improved and surprisingly lighter when not working within the framework of the parent band. Of course, he and Stanley were largely the architects of these constraints in the first place, so it is on them for limiting Kiss and arguably preventing them from becoming a more multi-faceted band. Considering their success, perhaps they felt they only needed one string on their collective bow, but as Irving Berlin so wisely warned, 'There may be trouble ahead….'

Gene Simmons gained the highest chart position of the four, peaking at 22, although *Ace Frehley* outsold it in the long run. The press was largely favourable, although *Sounds*' resident Kiss champion Geoff Barton and *Rolling Stone*'s Robert Duncan both big up the songs that sound most like Kiss while bemoaning those that don't, perhaps forgetting that the point of the solo album was to allow the bassist to spread his batwings.

Paul Stanley

Personnel:

Paul Stanley: lead vocals, backing vocals, rhythm guitar, lead guitar, acoustic guitar, EBow, all guitars on 'Hold Me, Touch Me (Think of Me When We're Apart)'

Bob Kulick: lead guitar, acoustic guitar

Steve Buslowe: bass guitar on tracks 1- 5

Eric Nelson: bass guitar on tracks 6- 9

Richie Fontana: drums on track 1- 4

Carmine Appice: drums on 'Take Me away (Together as One)'

Craig Krampf: drums on tracks 6- 9

Diana Grasseli, Miriam Naomi Valle, Maria Vidal: backing vocals on 'Move On'

Peppy Castro: backing vocals on 'Ain't Quite Right' and 'Hold Me, Touch Me (Think

of Me When We're Apart)'
Doug Katsaros: piano, Omni string ensemble and backing vocals on 'Hold Me, Touch Me (Think of Me When We're Apart)'
Steve Lacey: electric guitar on 'Love in Chains'
Produced at Electric Lady and the record Plant, New York City, and the Village Recorder Studio, Los Angeles, February-July 1978
Produced by: Paul Stanley and Jeff Glixman
Released: 18 September 1978
Running time: 35.10
Highest chart place: US: 40
Tracklisting: 1. 'Tonight You Belong to Me' (Stanley) 4.41, 2. 'Move On' (Stanley, Japp) 3.12, 3. 'Ain't Quite Right' (Stanley, Japp) 3.34, 4. 'Wouldn't You Like to Know Me' (Stanley) 3.16, 5. 'Take Me Away (Together as One)' (Stanley, Japp) 5.26, 6. 'It's Alright' (Stanley) 3.38, 7. 'Hold Me, Touch Me (Think of Me When We're Apart)' (Stanley) 3.40, 8. 'Love in Chains' (Stanley) 3.34, 9. 'Goodbye' (Stanley) 4.09

Paul Stanley's solo record has oft been called the most Kiss-like of the four, hardly a surprise as he was always the band's primary songwriter and principal driving force. He wasn't a frustrated white soul singer like Criss, an out-and-out rocker like Frehley, or out to prove how multi-layered / unfocused (delete as appropriate) he was, which seems to have been Simmons' goal. The songs he wrote for Kiss were precisely the type of songs he wanted to write, so it makes sense that he wouldn't stray from that template here. *Paul Stanley*, therefore, benefits from its creator's ability to spin great riffs and hooks, and from some highly polished production from the Starchild himself. Jeff Glixman, who by this point had produced four albums for Kansas, including their best-selling *Point of Know Return*, is also credited as producer, but according to Chris Lendt, he and Stanley didn't see eye-to-starry-eye, and they parted company. Thanks to the terms of his contract Glixman got paid and credited, although he only co-produced four tracks.

Speaking of riffs and hooks, 'Tonight You Belong to Me' has 'em. It starts with a twelve and six-string acoustic duet, a brushed cymbal or two, and some sweet crooning before some electric riffing assaults the left ear, and another lays siege to the right, drums and bass kick in, and we're off. He played the same trick two years earlier with 'I Want You', but 'Tonight You Belong to Me' is more expansive, presumably benefitting from time off from the road after so many years. In its own way, it is as rollicking an album opener as Frehley's 'Rip It Out.'

Bob Kulick, who had lost out to Ace at the auditions and who subbed for him on the *Alive II* studio tracks, returns to play lead throughout Stanley's album.

'Move On' is strictly so-so and sounds like a pre-*Destroyer* song, although it was specifically written for the solo. It is partly enlivened by the trio of Diana Grasseli, Miriam Naomi Valle, and Maria Vidal on backing vocals, all of whom were then members of Desmond Child and Rouge. Vidal went on to have a solo career and an international hit with 'Body Rock' in 1984, while Child would enter the Kiss story with 1979's *Dynasty* album.

Stanley's co-writer on this song was Mikal Japp, a Welsh musician who had previously been a touring member of Marmalade and would collaborate with John Waite on some material for the Babys. He would later cop a co-writer's credit for songs on the *Killers* partial compilation album and *Creatures of the Night*.

'Ain't Quite Right' was the first song Stanley and Japp wrote together, and with its scratchy, sparse arrangement and jazz-lite affectations, it is the furthest Paul would get from the current Kiss sound. Bassist Steve Buslowe can be heard to great effect here, and indeed on all the tracks that comprised side one. At the time, the young bassist was a member of Meat Loaf's touring band, a position he would retain for two decades, eventually becoming Mr. Loaf's musical director. Despite his obvious talent (check out his playing on 'Tonight You Belong to Me'), he admits that Stanley had to teach him the bass part for this song, note for note.

'Wouldn't You Like to Know Me' is a power-pop classic, no surprise considering it is an affectionate and convincing tribute to Cleveland's finest, the Raspberries, and draws inspiration from their songs 'Tonight' and 'Ecstasy', with just a hint of 'Go All the Way'. The polished mask of professionalism slips a bit here, and this sounds like a bunch of musicians having fun. Despite Kulick's assertion that they nailed it in five minutes (*Behind the Mask*), it is the highlight of the album and one of Stanley's all-time best.

'Take Me Away (Together as One)' is Japp's final co-write, a power ballad with huge crunching guitar chords and epic drum fills on the chorus, the latter courtesy of Carmine Appice, formerly of Vanilla Fudge and Beck, Bogert & Appice. Appice seems intent in dragging the song out of AOR territory with percussion that starts over the top and builds from there. If the meme had existed then, this would be Appice's 'I'm an Anteater!' moment.

For side two, Stanley switched coasts and rhythm sections; out went New York, Steve Buslowe (bass) and Richie Fontana (drums), and in came Los Angeles, with Eric Nelson and Craig Kampf on bass and drums, respectively. Bob Kulick remained on lead guitar. None of these changes affected the quality of the opening track, 'It's Alright', another song in which Stanley displays his power pop chops to hard rocking effect. It was the second last to be completed and was added as Stanley felt the album lacked 'an up-tempo, kick-ass rock 'n' roll song' (*Behind the Mask*).

In 1978 Dave Marshall was the breakfast DJ on Radio Clyde, a relatively new commercial radio station which served the city of Glasgow and its environs. Like breakfast shows the world over, Marshall's show featured the news, traffic, and weather interspersed with the occasional song. Tracks like David Soul's 'Silver Lady', Brian and Michael's 'Matchstalk Men and Matchstalk Cats and Dogs', and 'Sandy' by John Travolta were Dave's forte. And 'Hold Me, Touch Me (Think of Me When We're Apart)', which Dave introduced as 'the new one from Paul Stanley', as if there had been a previous one. But Dave called it right in making this song his Record of the Week; it was exactly the sort of inoffensive, easy listening twaddle that gently eased the sleepy listener into their working day. Despite Dave's best efforts, it flopped, both in Glasgow and the rest of the known universe.

Fortunately, 'Love in Chains' comes in all guns a-blazing, or at least guitars a-squealing and riffs a-riffing, to chase the MOR blues away. Steve Lacey, who had previously appeared on Simmons' 'Radioactive' and was now filling in for an unavailable Kulick, provides a screaming, death-from-above guitar solo, possibly the album's best, and Kampf's drumming is just perfect. Lyrically, the song is not remotely as pervy as the title suggests.

And so to the final song, the aptly titled 'Goodbye', a gorgeous guitar-fest like many a song on the album. And like many a song on the album, not to mention a slew of Kiss numbers such as 'Anything for My Baby', 'Mr. Speed', 'I Stole Your Love', and 'Tomorrow and Tonight,' 'Goodbye' once again suggests power pop rather than hard rock is Stanley's true metier.

There may be a lighter touch at play on *Paul Stanley*, but as previously stated, it was the most Kissy of the four solos; strange then that it underperformed in comparison to the rest. It peaked at number 40, three places above *Peter Criss*, but surprisingly short of *Ace Frehley* and *Gene Simmons*, both of which breached the top thirty. Stanley's effort also enjoyed the least chart action, clocking up an eighteen-week residency, compared to stays of twenty for Criss, twenty-two for Simmons and twenty-three weeks for Frehley.

Billy Altman in *The Village Voice* was scathing, calling *Paul Stanley* 'Very bad Kiss. No memorable vocals, no memorable songs, and plenty of used riffs.' This sounds like an inexplicably harsh conclusion, but then Altman says, 'The highlight is 'Hold Me, Touch Me (Think of Me When We're Apart)', a mellow tune that deserves someone like Joey Travolta to do it justice', and suddenly Altman's judgemental skill becomes disposably suspect. Clearly, Billy only listened to breakfast radio at the time. Those in favour include *Sounds*' Geoff Barton, who, it will be remembered, thought it would be the best of the bunch if not for Frehley, while John Swenson of *Rolling Stone* agreed with the consensus that Stanley's record was closest to Kiss, but, in direct contrast to Altman, argued 'that his songs have more dynamic range than the group's work'.

Neil Bogart had originally envisioned Casablanca releasing two million copies of the solo albums, that is, 500,000 copies of each. But based on the contract agreed on New Year's Day 1977, the record company were honour-bound to release twice that amount. Bogart, ever the gambler, decided not only to rise to the occasion but go beyond it; Casablanca would release 1.25 million of each solo. It also printed limited edition picture discs of each album that sold so well they quickly released some more, somewhat less limited picture discs.

The release of the solo albums was also supported by the biggest marketing campaign ever conducted by a record company, as detailed by Larry Harris in *And Party Every Day*:

> We supplied retailers with half a million white plastic bags printed with the four solo album covers, along with an assortment of point-of-purchase displays and foam board signs. Hundreds upon hundreds of lavish press kits went out. We spent $1.2 million on ad buys in various forms of media. We bought sixty-second radio spots on over one hundred stations nationwide. We placed expensive thirty-second spots on youth-orientated prime-time TV shows like *Happy Days* and *Laverne and Shirley*. There were bus and subway ads in Manhattan, as well as billboards there and in L. A. We did four digital ads – one for each album – on the nineteen-month-old Jumbo Tron in Times Square.

Harris's summation of the albums' performance is withering. Casablanca was 'royally screwed', and Gene and Paul's records were 'miserable failures, as was Peter's effort'. This sounds harsh, as all albums bar Criss's did enter the top forty, and he was only a few places short, and they were all gold records, having sales of over half a million each. But as Chris Lendt explains in *Kiss and Sell*, 'The industry works on the basis of expectations. If you press five million records, you are expected to sell that many; otherwise, you have failed'.

Casablanca had banked on all four doing the same business as *Love Gun*, but it took all four solos combined to equal that album's sales. The record company had shipped platinum records but had only sold gold (This ludicrous mechanism whereby an album was certified based on how many units it shipped was soon scrapped in favour of measuring an album's success according to sales). They had spent a fortune on production, printing, promoting, and distribution, but it hadn't paid off. Retailers were either returning the solo albums in their hundreds of thousands, or they were dumping them in the discount bins. Super Kiss was off to a bad start, and it was about to get worse.

Kiss Meets the Phantom of the Park was broadcast by NBC on 28 October. The plot, such as it is, smacks of Hanna-Barbera's usual animated fare, the only missing ingredient being a character that says 'zoiks!' A mad scientist, Abner Devereux, is peeved that the owner of the amusement park at which he works is spending money on staging a Kiss concert, rather than on funding his animatronic figures for the park. Naturally, he decides to replace Kiss with robotic doubles that will incite the kids attending the concert to destroy the park. However, this is the comic book version of Kiss, complete with talismans and powers, so they fight back, admittedly none too strenuously, and save the day.

It is a movie that stays in the mind for all the wrong reasons, and any viewer might find themselves springing awake in the middle of the night asking dumb questions like, 'Why do Kiss suddenly have superpowers?' Kiss fans would know, because they would have bought the comic books, but John Q. Public must have been mystified. For that matter, why is the villain called the Phantom of the Park in the title? He lives and works beneath an amusement park in the film, which is a far from crystal clear nod to the Phantom beneath the Paris Opera House in Gaston Leroux's classic novel, but unlike that situation, there is no mystery here. Everyone knows where Devereux lives, and everyone knows his name. It's Abner. And isn't designing animatronic figures for an amusement park a little too underachieving for a mad scientist? King of all the midnight questions, however, is this: was Paul Stanley really eavesdropping using his *eye*?

There is a damsel in distress, played by Deborah Ryan, whose boyfriend has gone missing in the amusement park, so Kiss agree to help find him by sitting around a pool singing 'Beth'. It is stripped down from the orchestrated *Destroyer* version to just Peter on vocals, Paul on acoustic guitar, and Gene and Ace on looking contemplative and stoned, respectively. It marks the only time Criss's voice is heard in the movie, as his drug and alcohol intake made his naturally thick Brooklynese even more indiscernible, so his lines were overdubbed by a voice actor (either Michael Bell or Norman Alden, yet another 'depending on who you read' scenario). Simmons sometimes sounds like he has been dubbed by the MGM lion, while the rest of the time his voice is electronically distorted, which makes him sound more robotic than demonic.

Hanna-Barbera co-founder Joseph Barbera thought, 'It was a heck of a picture', and particularly enjoyed the scene 'when those white monkeys started climbing up the roller coaster'. He was in the minority. Here's Chris Lendt describing the screening party for the film:

> The mood was festive, and while the movie was airing, everyone cheered Kiss on, laughing at all the right moments, and applauding feverishly at the end. When the house lights went up, smiles flashed and endless rounds of congratulations and accolades were heaped on Kiss. A fun time was had by all, except Kiss. Paul and Gene had a glazed look in their eyes and Peter was strangely subdued, almost withdrawn.

Referring to the same screening in *Face the Music*, Stanley wrote, 'If you thought it was bad on the TV screen, you should have seen it on the big screen! People openly laughed. I slunk down in my seat. It was humiliating. The finished film was absolutely awful'. In *Makeup to Breakup*, Criss opined that 'All of us were ultimately embarrassed by doing that movie. The reviews were uniformly horrible. We actually got a lot of hate mail from fans after that movie'. In an early-Nineties magazine interview, Simmons compared the movie to *Plan 9 from Outer Space*, generally regarded as the worst movie of all time. Only Frehley seemed to take it in his stride, writing in *No Regrets*, 'I didn't really take it seriously from the outset and I didn't think much about it once it was over'.

Criss was right about the reviews, with *The Los Angeles Times* speaking for most when they proclaimed the movie 'a four-star abomination ... A five-minute idea for a cartoon disguised as a two-hour TV movie'.

The movie became The Great Unmentionable around the members of Kiss for years to come. The band, or more accurately Stanley and Simmons, lay the blame at Bill Aucoin's feet. It caused the first major crack to form between band and manager and marked the beginning of the end of their relationship.

Kiss Meets the Phantom of the Park was always going to be a made-for-TV movie, but Kiss were also offered the chance to make their big screen debut that same year. They were approached to appear as the Future Villain Band in the film *Sgt. Pepper's Lonely Hearts Club Band*, which starred the Bee Gees and Peter Frampton, but turned it down as they didn't want to be seen as the bad guys. The role went to Aerosmith, and the movie went on to become a box office bomb, with David Ansen of *Newsweek* memorably calling it 'a film with a dangerous resemblance to wallpaper'. The movie's poor performance had no notable impact on Aerosmith, but they weren't already mortally wounded like Kiss following the TV movie and the solo albums debacle.

1979: Dynasty

Dynasty

Personnel:

Paul Stanley: rhythm guitar, vocals, lead guitar on 'Sure Know Something' and 'Magic Touch', bass on 'I Was Made for Loving You' and 'Magic Touch'

Ace Frehley: lead guitar, vocals, all guitars and bass on '2000 Man', 'Hard Times', and 'Save Your Love'

Gene Simmons: bass, vocals, rhythm guitar on 'X-Ray Eyes'

Peter Criss: drums, vocals on 'Dirty Livin''

Additional personnel:

Anton Fig: drums on all tracks except 'Dirty Livin''

Vini Poncia: keyboards, percussion, backing vocals

Recorded at Electric Lady and Record Plant Studios, New York City, January-February 1979

Produced by: Vini Poncia

Released: 23 May 1979

Running time: 39.19

Highest chart places: US: 9, UK: 50

Tracklisting: 1. 'I Was Made for Lovin' You' (Stanley, Poncia, Child) 4.30, 2. '2,000 Man' (Jagger, Richards) 4.54, 3. 'Sure Know Something' (Stanley, Poncia) 4.00, 4. 'Dirty Livin'' (Criss, Penridge) 4.27, 5. 'Charisma' (Simmons, Marks) 4.25, 6. 'Magic Touch' (Stanley) 4.41, 7. 'Hard Times' (Frehley) 3.30, 8. 'X-Ray Eyes' (Simmons) 3.46, 9. 'Save Your Love' (Frehley) 4.41

The twin autumn offensive of the solo albums and the TV movie, plus Gene Simmons' regular appearances in the celebrity press with new girlfriend Cher, meant that Kiss were still very much in the spotlight, but plans were well underway when 1979 began for what was being billed as 'the Return of Kiss'. It had been a year and a half since the last studio album by the band and nearly a year since their last concert proper on American soil. Rock bands release albums and play shows, and it was time for Kiss to get back to the meat and potatoes of rock and roll.

But 'Kiss is no longer just a rock group', confided Gene Simmons to Chris Lendt, 'Only Paul thinks it's still a rock group', So, what *exactly* was Kiss? Simmons set Lendt straight. 'Kiss had transcended the world of rock 'n' roll. We had now entered the era of an institutional Kiss where Kiss's influence would emanate like rays into every aspect of pop culture, media, and entertainment. Kiss could do everything and anything; they were omnipotent and omniscient'. The last thing they wanted to do as they returned to their day job was just put on a show; it had to be 'the mother of all shows'. The 'show of shows'. The 'ultimate concert'. To use Lendt's own terminology, Kiss were still in the process of metamorphosising into Super Kiss.

There would be a new stage set, sleek, modern, and vast. It would have multiple levels, and runways that reached out into the audience. The lighting and sound systems would redefine the state of the art. Hydraulic systems would allow the band to descend upon the stage like gods from on high, each bathed in their signature colour. Each band member would have their own special effects. Peter Criss's drum riser would no longer simply levitate as in the past; that was too old hat. Instead, it would be able to roam the stage, rotating, moving forwards, backwards and to the sides. For the first time, Simmons would 'fly', via a harness, to the top of the light rig to belt out 'God of Thunder'. Frehley would retain his trademark smoking guitar, but now, mid-solo, he would let it go and it would 'levitate' into the air, still smoking, while the Space Ace strapped on another guitar that fired rockets, which he would use to blow up the one floating skywards. Stanley would wear a special eyepiece that would allow him to shoot laser beams from his eye. All bar the last made it to the finished stage show, the eyepiece ultimately abandoned for safety reasons.

Another new addition would be a laser show, which both Blue Oyster Cult and the Electric Light Orchestra had been deploying to spectacular effect. In fact, at a production meeting in February, Criss had been against the laser idea, suggesting that what ELO presented would be difficult to beat. He was over-ruled on the basis that 'the Kiss show will be the most exciting show on the road, and any form of competition will not affect them'. Why listen to the drug-addled drummer, right? As it turns out, he *was* right. The laser show, which cost an astonishing quarter of a million dollars to build, failed on opening night, and was promptly dropped. Kiss spent years tied up in litigation trying to get their money back.

Even without the lasers, the costs of the stage show were astronomical. In *Kiss and Sell*, Lendt says it cost 'hundreds of thousands of dollars in start-up costs just to bring the show into Nassau Community College (where rehearsals for the tour would take place) and hundreds of thousands of dollars once more once we set up there'. According to *Billboard*, the Kiss show had start-up costs of $2.2 million, and that figure would soon be swamped once the costs of transport, set-up, running, and strike for each date were factored in. Furthermore, someone in the

Kiss organisation decided it would be prudent to build two stages, which would leapfrog each other as Kiss worked their way around the country. While they were playing in City A, another crew could be hard at work setting the second stage up in Town B.

The itinerary and venue selection were other new considerations, both of which were decided upon specifically to offset the exorbitant costs of the stage show. Setting up and striking the stage every night was not economically or logistically viable, so the decision was taken that Kiss would play two or more consecutive nights in the same venue, and that, to further maximise sales and increase efficiency, the concerts would only be staged in the country's biggest arenas and stadiums. Additionally, the stage would sit in the middle of the venues with the drums in the centre, with staging and ramps both at the front and back of the riser. This would allow Kiss to perform in the round, which conveniently would allow sales of seating that would normally be closed off to accommodate the traditional placing of the stage at one end of the venue.

All this was truly shaping up to be 'the mother of all shows', but then Gene Simmons had a brainwave: Kiss World. This would be a travelling amusement park, Kiss-themed of course, that would be erected next to the venues that the band would play. It would have the expected rollercoasters, thrill rides, side shows, and attractions, a movie theatre showing Kiss-related films, a Madame Tussauds-style wax museum featuring the fantastic foursome in character-befitting dioramas, and a Kiss museum consisting of previous costumes, sets and other memorabilia, not to mention circus acts such as clowns, trapeze artists, magicians, a ringmaster, and the like. And there would be many merchandise stands dotted throughout.

Stanley was dubious. The only member of the band who still thought of Kiss as a rock and roll band didn't think Kiss World sounded very rock and roll, but the Kiss World concept forged ahead until, suddenly, it didn't. Several factors put paid to the plan. First were the obvious economic factors of hiring everything from the rides and portable cinemas to fencing and power cables, not to mention the costs of the necessary expertise and hands-on decks. Second were the logistical problems, the most notable being that few of the proposed venues had sufficient adjacent space to accommodate a travelling theme park, or if they did it would be at the cost of the car parking space, making it difficult for customers travelling to either the concert or Kiss World. And finally, there were the promoters, none of whom were particularly thrilled about the Kiss World concept. The costs to them would be great, and the risk unproportionally greater. Sales forecasts for other acts hitting the summer circuit weren't promising, and promoters were already worried about how many Kiss tickets they would be able to sell without factoring in the additional headache a travelling theme park would entail.

Kiss, of course, had no such worries because they had transcended the old rules. By playing consecutive nights at high-capacity venues, they had a strategy that maximised sales while bypassing the costly another night, another city tour model. Furthermore, they were at the peak of their powers, pop culture icons with a spectacular new show, new costumes, and a new album in the works. What could possibly go wrong?

Alongside the tour preparations, the band spent the beginning of the year recording that new album, which was to be called *Dynasty*, a title that had been kicking around since the *Destroyer* days. Criss pulled another of his 'do this or I quit' routines when he demanded that the new album be produced by Vini Poncia, who Peter had worked with on his solo record. Bill Aucoin also backed the choice of Poncia, seeing it as a way to placate Criss and hopefully reverse his increasing dissatisfaction and detachment from the band. Criss got his way, but it backfired on him as one of Poncia's first decisions was to replace him on the drum kit. Criss's drumming ability had deteriorated as his substance abuse increased, and Poncia decided he was no longer up to the job. Instead, he hired Anton Fig, who had played on Ace's solo album. Surprisingly, the normally short-fused Criss acquiesced, such was his personal despondency and antipathy towards the band. 'I didn't feel betrayed', he wrote in *Makeup to Breakup*. 'I was happy they got him. I didn't really want to play with them anymore'. In the end, Criss would contribute only to the track he co-authored, 'Dirty Livin''.

Despite being part of the whole 'Return of Kiss' programme, *Dynasty* ultimately demonstrated that this was a band on the verge of disintegration. Criss was all but gone, but even Simmons was only a part-timer on the album, as Frehley played bass on his own songs, with Stanley doing likewise on two of his tracks, 'Sure Know Something' and 'Magic Touch'. That leaves Simmons only contributing to four of the album's nine tracks, and the jury is still out on whether he played on 'I Was Made for Lovin' You'. Meanwhile, Frehley also dispensed with Stanley, playing all guitars on his three songs, while Stanley did his own guitar solo on 'Sure Know Something.'

Bill Aucoin hired renowned fashion photographer Francesco Scavullo, best known for his many *Vogue* and *Cosmopolitan* covers, for the album cover shoot. As well as his work for the glossies, Scavullo was responsible for the iconic movie poster/album cover for the 1976 version of *A Star is Born*, as well as a couple of Donna Summer albums. Scavullo not only shot superstars but was considered one himself, so only an artist of his stature could be considered for Super Kiss.

Art director Dennis Woloch's cover concept flew in the face of reality insofar as he wanted to depict a band united. Chris Lendt states in *Kiss and Sell* that the *Dynasty* cover was like a laborious jigsaw for Woloch. Because the members of Kiss didn't approve any one image of themselves, the art director created the finished artwork by selecting bits and pieces from the hundreds of photos taken and stitched them together into an idealised whole. Woloch says this is an exaggeration. His memory is that only Stanley was particularly fussy about how he looked, so his face comes from one photo shoot while the other three faces come from another. Even then, there was some retouching done to Stanley's image, taking his hair from one shot, and putting it onto another. Meanwhile, Simmons pulls a face that exposes his bottom teeth, a common pose for him in the late Seventies as he had braces on his upper teeth.

The cover shots were done relatively quickly, so with time to kill on the $40,000 photo shoot tour manager Fritz Postlethwaite was dispatched to Bellvue psychiatric hospital to get straitjackets for some further photographs. Pictures taken during this impromptu session later provided the shot used for both the poster insert and the record's label, although Aucoin had the straitjackets airbrushed over as he felt they had negative connotations.

The album was released on 23 May, with the first single, 'I Was Made for Lovin' You' preceding it by three days. *Rolling Stone*'s David Fricke predicted that 'The Kiss Army is going to mutiny when they hear 'I Was Made for Lovin' You', the disco-inflected leadoff track on the Masked Marvels' latest album', but was anyone really surprised considering the number of rock acts that had already dabbled in the genre? Former glam supremos T. Rex were probably first to bridge the divide with 1975's 'Dreamy Lady' single, which was even credited to T. Rex Disco Party. More significantly that year, the Bee Gees tested the waters with 'Jive Talkin'' before morphing into full-time floor-filling behemoths, starting with 'You Should Be Dancing' in 1976. The floodgates opened, and although Frank Zappa and The Tubes satirised the genre with 'Disco Boy' and 'Slipped

My Disco', respectively, they were smart enough to give the music some serious beats. Other rockers tried their hand, from Alice Cooper with '(No More) Love at Your Convenience', to the Rolling Stones with 'Miss You' and Rod Stewart with 'Do Ya Think I'm Sexy'. In 1979 alone, Blondie ('Heart of Glass'), ELO ('Shine a Little Love') Paul McCartney and Wings ('Goodnight Tonight'), and Sparks ('The Number One Song in Heaven' and 'Beat the Clock') all threw their hats into that illuminated tiled dance floor. Furthermore, Kiss were on Casablanca who, thanks to their success with Donna Summer, the Village People, and Parliament/Funkadelic, amongst others, were now selling themselves as the home of disco, so their prime signing doing a dance track should have come as a shock to precisely no one.

That said, there were those that saw Kiss releasing a disco song as a further step away from what they perceived the band to be, and their dislike of the song was echoed by every member of the band that didn't have a hand in writing it. Simmons hated it, thought it 'too girly', and felt that all the 'do-do-dos' made him sing like his grandmother. Frehley said, 'I could appreciate the polish behind it, but I never liked the song and frankly hated playing it live – hammering that chuka-chuka-chuka chord for five minutes straight was not only monotonous but often gave me a cramp in my wrist'. Criss suggests 'what little credibility we had left was flushed down the toilet when we did that'.

Despite its naysayers, 'I Was Made for Lovin' You' is the band's most successful single. It reached the top of the charts in Belgium, Canada, France, the Netherlands, and New Zealand and hit number two in Australia, South Africa, and West Germany. It peaked at a very respectable eleven on the *Billboard* chart, earning the band their second (and final) gold disc for a single, and it even tickled the chart in the Kiss-disinclined United Kingdom by hitting number 50, their first and only top fifty hit of the Seventies in that country.

Stanley shared songwriting credits with producer Poncia and Desmond Child, who would cowrite regularly with Kiss's frontman throughout the 1980s, contributing to the albums *Animalize*, *Asylum*, *Crazy Nights*, *Smashes, Thrashes & Hits*, and *Hot in the Shade*.

Despite Peter Criss's appearance in the promotional video for 'I Was Made For Love' You,' it was Anton Fig who drummed on this and all other tracks bar 'Dirty Livin''.

Frehley brought in a demo of the Rolling Stones song '2000 Man', which he thought 'spacey' enough to suit his character, to the sessions, and it was considered well-produced enough to go on the album as is. As a result, Frehley played all guitars on the song, including bass. It is a good cover, Ace's buzzsaw guitar cutting through the post-Summer of Love dreaminess of the original, but his solo album had bolstered both his confidence and his songwriting, so an original song would have been a more satisfying inclusion, especially when two, 'Backstage Pass' and 'Insufficient Data,' were on the same demo tape as '2000 Man'. Presumably, these failed to pass the Stanley-Simmons quality control test. Kiss revisited the Stones' song when joined by Frehley at the 1995 *MTV Unplugged* show, but it was a poor choice and hardly indicative of the guitarist's work.

'Sure Know Something', by Stanley and Poncia, might not be the disco assault 'I Was Made For Lovin' You' was, but with its polished R&B grooves and a down and dirty bassline it is undeniably danceable. It is perhaps no surprise then that it was released as the second single from the album, but it failed to match its illustrious predecessor's success, cracking the top ten in only two territories, and stalling at 47 in the States.

'Dirty Livin'' is a Criss-Penridge coproduction, and – surprise! – it dates from the Lips days. By this point, Criss was utterly dissatisfied with his role in Kiss and seriously contemplating his solo career, but how he thought he could sustain it when he was forever returning to the same ancient well for material is symptomatic of how delusional he was at the time. He did bring another three songs to the sessions, although how current they were is unknown. Presumably 'Dirty Livin'' was considered the best of the bunch, but it is a poor fit that is crying out for a horn section.

The fact that it takes until side two before a Gene Simmons song crops up is further demonstration of the bassist's declining interest in the day job. As the Eighties loomed, Simmons was more interested in producing other acts and getting into the movies. As far as the band were concerned, he had been there, done that. That said, 'Charisma' is a corker, full of buzzsaw guitars, demonic vocalising, and some great percussive work from Fig. Lyrically, Gene ponders why women are attracted to him, wondering whether it is down to his personality or his sexuality, his body or his brain, or his fortune or his fame, to which the answer is no, no, no, no, yes, and yes.

''Magic Touch' was a great song', says Stanley modestly in *Behind the Mask*, 'that unfortunately got mucked up when it was recorded, as did a lot of songs on *Dynasty* and *Unmasked*'. Uh-oh. Sounds like Vini Poncia is getting scapegoated for something, but if you hire a producer for their sound, then you can hardly blame them when they deliver. For the record, 'Magic Touch' is a so-so song, the least of Stanley's three contributions to the album, the only 'great' bit being the vocals at the bridge.

Frehley's 'Hard Times' is an autobiographical song loosely describing his late high school years. Typical of Frehley's work at the time, this rocker has a memorable riff, a killer solo, and some shouty lyrics. 'Hard Times' is essentially a solo record as the only players are him and Anton Fig, and indeed it was originally floated for his 1978 album. It would prove to be a nice little earner for Frehley when it was placed on the B-side of 'I Was Made for Lovin' You'.

'X-Ray Eyes' is Simmons' second and last song on the album, a real change from the pre-solo days when he was as prolific a contributor as Stanley. However, perhaps not feeling the pressure to come up with roughly half an album benefitted the bassist, as 'X-Ray Eyes' is a strong, metal-edged pop song that acts as a nice counterbalance to some of the album's more polished elements.

The album closes with Frehley's 'Save Your Love', which makes this the first Kiss album where the guitarist's contribution has been equal to Stanley's and greater than Simmons'. The Space Ace had well and truly landed. 'Save Your Love' is full of the usual rock 'n' riffery and boasts an album-best performance from Fig, but things take a wonderful turn for the bonkers once the chorus arrives, whereupon the backing vocalists chant the title like extras from a Hammer horror film, an imaginary movie called *Knights in Satan's Service*, perhaps? It certainly sounds like Eugene the Demon is in there, but Stanley's vocal contribution once the song hits the fade is unmistakable, but as he didn't have any other involvement, this was presumably another ploy of Aucoin's to give the illusion of unity.

It might have contained a couple of wobbles, but if *Dynasty* marked 'the return of Kiss' then it did so in fine style. Naturally, the critics disagreed. *Rolling Stone* didn't like the album – no surprise there! – with reviewer David Fricke pinning the blame on producer Poncia, claiming he had 'smothered the fire' of the classic Kiss sound with a 'sorry lack of spark' and timid production. The sporadically supportive *Creem*, in the shape of Jeffrey Morgan, felt the band had strayed too far from their hard rock roots and suggested they 'leave the pop diddlings to Abba and the disco stuff to Giorgio Moroder'. *Dynasty* was a commercial smash, however, returning Kiss to the *Billboard* top ten. It reached pole position in the Netherlands, number two in Australia, New Zealand, and France, and the top ten in Germany and Canada.

New costumes were required for the upcoming tour, so Bill Aucoin went all Hollywood and hired Peter Manefee. Manefee had started his career as a dancer – he's one of the chimney sweeps singing 'Step In Time' in *Mary Poppins* – but had moved on to costume design by the 1970s. By the time he got the Kiss gig, his resumé included television specials for Bing Crosby, Jack Benny, Perry Como, Shirley MacLaine, Barry Manilow, and Olivia Newton John. All this should have set alarm bells ringing, but if it did, no one was listening. Manefee's costumes would be unveiled to the public on the first date of the tour, and, boy, were they ugly.

The most obvious change was the ditching of the traditional jet and silver in favour of outfits that incorporated the individual colours from the solo albums. Simmons got off lightest, his costume a vaguely organic variation of the *Destroyer* armour with added crimson cape. Frehley's maintained the V-shaped torso evident in the *Hotter than Hell*, *Destroyer* and *Love Gun* outfits, but now it was ridiculously exaggerated, as were his gauntlets. These elements of his costume, and the boots, were now metallic blue interspersed with mirrors to reflect the stage lights. The worst addition was his cape, a flouncy, pleated, silver-blue shower curtain. Speaking of monstrosities, Stanley now wore a pink (or lavender, as he generously describes it in his book) jacket that seemed to have as many holes as it did material. It made him look like some fairy prince, or at least some glammed-up Elizabethan actor playing one. And finally, there was Peter Criss's costume, which was so hideously embarrassing he could probably have won a case of constructive dismissal. He was draped in the pelts of two emerald lions, their faces resting on his shoulders and staring lovingly / loathingly / it's hard to tell at his face. Encircling his legs beneath the knees are the carcasses of many a slaughtered small green mammal – species unknown, possibly prairie dogs. He looks lost in the photographs of him wearing this costume, as if trying to fathom when he became a gamma-irradiated Ted Nugent.

Criss and Stanley dumped the green fur and sweet prince trappings almost as soon as they hit the stage, and Frehley and Simmons would divest themselves of their cloaks mid-set, all of which begs the question, what was the point? The outfits were garish, later variously described as 'Vegas', 'Disney', or 'H. R. Pufnstuf on Ice' by band members, and to conceive of them at a time when the charts were dominated by skinny tie bands like the Pretenders, Blondie, and the Cars shows how out of touch everyone on Planet Kiss was.

These sartorial nightmares were meant to be unveiled to the public on the first day of the tour in Lakeland, Florida, but it was cancelled. As per their Super Kiss itinerary, the 10,000-seat capacity Civic Centre had been booked for two shows, but only 8,000 tickets, or forty per cent, had been sold in total. It was an ominous start to the tour, made more so when the same fate befell the second date in Savannah six days later, with the demand here even less. The *Savannah Morning News* reported that only 700 tickets had been sold for the axed show. Meanwhile, July saw six of the planned twenty shows cancelled, including three of a proposed five-night residency at Madison Square Garden. Furthermore, some cities, such as Largo, Maryland were only shifting just over half the available tickets, and Asheville, North Carolina two-thirds. The nigh-universal sold-out success of the *Love Gun* tour now seemed a distant memory. However, it wasn't all bad news; Greenville, also in North Carolina, sold out 88% of its capacity, and Toronto 82%, and they were not alone. Additionally, the smaller venues, those in the 7,000-8,000 seat range, *were* selling out. Based on attendance figures, the tour looked like it was doing robust business, but with its extravagant costs, it was always just on the verge of breaking even, and now the string of cancelled dates put it in the red.

An emergency meeting was called. In attendance were the band and Bill Aucoin, their business managers Carl Glickman and Howard Marks, tour manager Fritz Postlethwaite, and several others representing business and logistics. The tour was haemorrhaging money, and the purpose of the meeting was to suggest solutions. It was suggested that Kiss play some of the smaller towns and cities, putting on a scaled-down version of their show, and this would offset the costs of the full-on super spectacular. Aucoin was incredulous. He was in the process of building up Super Kiss, and now the business team wanted to water them down? Kiss's reputation was built on their show; to 'scale it down' would be to reduce them, to turn them into Kansas, or Styx, or indeed any other band. Simmons and Stanley lent vociferous support. Kiss had to have the biggest stage, the best light show, the greatest amount of pyro, the most mountainous sound system. And they had to have their set pieces, Peter's roving drum riser, Gene's flying harness, Ace's rocket-shooting guitar. Also, playing smaller towns and cities? That's what they did in '75 and '76. Kiss didn't play Hicksville, USA, anymore.

The scaled-down proposal became the shot-down proposal. Kiss and Aucoin sanctioned the firing of the advance man, a gopher that ensured that the hotel rooms were ready and to the band's expected standard, and a police liaison whose job was to organise police accompaniment for Kiss as they shuttled between venue and hotel. Frehley agreed to pay his own champagne bill, approximately $1,000 a week, and Criss was willing to stump up for his own cigarettes. And that was it. A drop in the ocean that didn't so much save money as negligibly reduce the amount they lost. 'We were moving inexorably towards a day of reckoning somewhere down the line', wrote Lendt, 'and all of us bean counters knew it'.

On 30 June, a young band called New England joined the tour as Kiss's opening act. This Boston-based quartet already had a couple of Kiss connections, in that Paul Stanley produced their eponymous debut and Bill Aucoin was their manager. Aucoin's expanding roster of artists was another source of friction between him and Kiss, as Aucoin had not only taken on New England, but was also looking after Starz, Piper, Virgin, Toby Beau, Spider (featuring Anton Fig), and the Skatt Brothers (featuring Sean Delaney), all bands that went nowhere fast, but which distracted Aucoin from his primary charges. Kiss was also peeved that between his commission on their income and the money he raked in from merchandising, Aucoin was earning more than they were. Finally, they were still haunted by the *Phantom of the Park* fiasco, which, as far as they were concerned, was all Aucoin's fault.

In September, Aucoin's contract was up for renegotiation, and according to Criss, Glickman, Marks, Stanley, and Simmons all sensed blood. They landed a few verbal uppercuts regarding areas in which the manager's performance was not up to scratch, and Aucoin was on the ropes. At this point, the Catman stepped up, saying that although some of their points were valid, they should all remember that they were only where they were because of Aucoin and his American Express card. Frehley agreed with Criss's perspective, and Aucoin kept his job. Parts of his contract *were* renegotiated, but nothing that was lifestyle-threatening. However, the point had been made: Aucoin may have made them, but even his coat could hang on a shaky peg. The Kiss-Aucoin relationship may have been salvaged, but there was no saving Peter and Lydia Criss's marriage. Their divorce was finalised on 13 September.

Kiss played Tulsa, Oklahoma, on 30 October, then flew to New York to record an appearance on *Tomorrow with Tom Snyder*, which would be broadcast the following evening. This would become infamous in Kiss lore when a visibly hammered and wisecracking Frehley stole the show, much to the chagrin of Stanley and Simmons. Even as late as 2012, Stanley was telling *LA Weekly*:

> It may seem funny that somebody is drunk … but the fact is that the root of it was, I believe, a contempt and a lack of respect for the audience and the fans. So, sure, can you look at it and chuckle? Yeah. I can, too, but I see deeper. And I look at it and say, what a shame to take this lofty position that somebody gave us and spit on it. Spit in its face. By showing up inebriated or unable to connect a sentence. It may be funny on the surface, but what's below the surface is a lack of appreciation for the gift that you have been given.

Holy cow! Sounds like the Space Ace was bang out of order. So, what gross transgression did Frehley commit on Snyder's show? Well, he *was* drunk, but he was also coherent, quick-witted, and genuinely funny, and he never once appeared disrespectful. It was possibly the first interview where a member of Kiss acted naturally. He was also clearly more aware than Stanley, who at one point said, 'The very first tour we did, you know, you expect all these women, and you start settling for girls'. Despite Simmons seemingly whispering a not-so-coded warning ('True confessions time'), Stanley stumbled over further possible self-incriminatory statements before realisation apparently dawned and suddenly, his monologue took a left turn into a bog-standard rock 'n' roll tale about Ace ejecting hotel furniture out the window. Moreover, there is a strong case to be argued that charging fans an income-damaging $4,000 for a VIP package (as on the current *End of the Road* tour) shows a greater 'lack of appreciation for the gift that you have been given', especially coming from a band that repeatedly claim they do what they do 'for the fans'.

The next day Kiss flew out to Lubbock, Texas, to continue the tour, which also included dates in November and December. Chris Lendt, Paul Stanley, and Peter Criss all recount in their respective books how Criss 'sabotaged' the band's 8 December gig at Shreveport, Louisiana. 'Paul humiliated me in front of the audience in the same way he had done many times before', said Criss. Stanley's 'transgression', which he admits in *Face the Music*, was to indicate to Criss that his tempo was too fast; Criss adds that Stanley did this by lifting 'his arm in an exaggerated gesture'. In retaliation, Criss slowed right down during the song, leaving Stanley to gesticulate again wildly for him to up the tempo again. The bottom line is the show was cut short and there was no encore, meaning that fan favourites such as 'Beth' and 'Rock and Roll All Nite' were jettisoned.

There were more shenanigans from the drummer at the next concert, two days later in Jackson, Mississippi. Criss stopped playing during 'Move On' and left the stage without explanation. The band finished the song and followed him backstage, reappearing after fifteen minutes. Stanley told the crowd that Criss had been hit in the eye by a fragment of a broken drumstick and had left to seek medical attention. It was a good cover story, but one he could hardly repeat when Criss, sitting in front of the stage and far removed from his drum kit, again stormed off after singing 'Beth'.

At the concert after that, in Biloxi, Criss deliberately threw a drumstick at Simmons, an occupational hazard according to Stanley; 'It wasn't unusual for Peter to throw his drumsticks at me or Gene or Ace if we stepped in front of his drum riser.' This time the drumstick hit its target, leading to an altercation between the bassist and drummer backstage. Simmons kicked Criss in the shin, and Criss, the Brooklyn tough guy, said, 'it hurt with those gigantic boots'. In his autobiography, Criss claims to have then smashed one of Frehley's champagne bottles against the wall and lunged for Simmons, but was held back by members of the road crew. This sounds like a very serious incident, but no mention of it, or the Jackson, Mississippi debacle, crops up in any of the other memoirs.

The *Dynasty* tour finished at Toledo, Ohio, on 16 December, and was Criss's last concert with the band until his 1996 return. Reviews were mixed throughout the tour, but one common thread was the shifting demographic at a Kiss concert. Alabama's *Birmingham News*, for example, opined that 'Twelve thousand, eight hundred Birmingham children were 'robbed' of their allowances last night. Willing accomplices in the 'theft' were a legion of parents who either stuffed cotton in their ears and braved the Kiss concert or waited for three hours in cars outside while the kids saw the show'. *The Louisville Times* noted that. 'This was not the ordinary rock concert audience. There were parents and even grandparents. There were children small enough not to worry about school this morning'. *The Daily Nebraskan* noted that the Kiss crowd ranged 'in age from three-year-olds to somewhere past 30, divided between those that really wanted to be there, and the fathers, mothers, and chaperones who would most likely be the victims of some delightfully nasty prank if the four-foot-tall character in full Gene Simmons make-up next to them had not been allowed to see Kiss'. And finally, the *Dallas Morning News* described the show at Fort Worth as 'a circus for the young and the young at heart – but mostly the young. The very young. The very, very young'.

Even Stanley commented about this on the Snyder show, where he put a positive spin on it. However, he viewed it slightly differently in *Face the Music*:

> We had sanitised ourselves and were well on the way to extinguishing the fire that had propelled us so far. We stayed at a hotel opposite the Forum in L.A. when we played there, and I looked out the window and broke into a cold sweat because I saw so many kids and families standing in line. The line could just as easily have been for the circus… It was all wrong.

The Seventies ended with Kiss adrift. As Aucoin had hoped, the band were now a pop culture phenomenon, but they had also become a fun day out for all the family. The comic books and the movie had ultimately worked against them, diluting their image as a serious rock band. Early posters for the *Dynasty* tour featured a comic drawing of the band running forward in their ludicrous new costumes; it looked more like the ad for a Saturday morning cartoon rather than a concert poster. If Kiss grew their audience at all, it was only because one half had to be chaperoned.

Despite the Super Kiss aspirations, the 1979 tour was not as successful in terms of ticket sales as the *Love Gun* tour two years earlier. The consecutive dates in major venues hadn't paid off, and the cancelled dates and Kiss's reluctance to run with the B-concert idea meant that the tour lost money. The Super Kiss stage show, a monument to both the pride and the fall, was quietly mothballed. Some of its key components would be resurrected with the original band in 1996.

Meanwhile, the band itself was fractured. Their relationship with Bill Aucoin would never recover and would hit a new bump when the band's cut of the tour merchandise proved to be a pittance. If Kiss was still a band of brothers, then they were a dysfunctional family as their lack of unity when recording *Dynasty* revealed. Stanley still wanted the band to work, but Simmons was less invested as evidenced by his paltry two-song contribution to the recent album. He had moved from rock star to celebrity and Hollywood was calling, or so he believed. Frehley, who had been threatening to call it a day for the past two years, was bolstered by the success of his solo album and stepped into the vacuum created by Simmons' relative absence. Criss, too, had been threatening to leave, but despite his unhappiness, his chemical dependency, his one-song appearance on *Dynasty*, and his unreliable behaviour on the tour, he was miraculously still hanging in there. Certainly, Stanley and Simmons wanted him out, believing his recent onstage antics were a line crossed, and although Frehley agreed with them in principle, he and Aucoin wanted to give the drummer one more chance. Would the Catman jump, or would he be pushed? As 1980 dawned, it was anyone's guess.

However, 1979 still held one last hurrah. On 23 December, Peter married Debra Jensen in Los Angeles, with Aucoin as his best man. Ace, Paul, and Gene were all in attendance, but according to Chris Lendt, that was more through duty than desire, and that they 'were irritated about the whole affair, as if it were an imposition to attend'. They could hardly be blamed as two days before Christmas was indeed an imposition on anyone, and Criss's behaviour and attitude during the tour would hardly have endeared him to the rest. They were also friends with Lydia, who had been part of the Kiss family since day one, so conflicting loyalties could also have been at play.

1980: Unmasked and the Departure of Peter Criss

Unmasked

Personnel:
Paul Stanley: rhythm guitar, vocals, lead guitar on 'Shandi', guitar solo on 'Is That You?', and 'You're All That I Want', first guitar solo on 'What Makes the World Go Round', all guitars and bass on 'Tomorrow' and 'Easy as It Seems'
Ace Frehley: lead guitar, vocals, second guitar solo on 'What Makes the World Go Round', all guitars and bass on 'Talk to Me', 'Two Sides of the Coin', and 'Torpedo Girl'
Gene Simmons: bass, vocals, rhythm guitar on 'You're All That I Want'
Peter Criss: credited as a band member but does not appear on the album
Additional personnel:
Anton Fig: drums
Vini Poncia: keyboards, percussion, backing vocals
Tom Harper: bass on 'Shandi'
Holly Knight: keyboards
Bob Kulick: additional guitar
Recorded at the Record Plant, New York City, January-March 1980
Produced by: Vini Poncia
Released: 20 May 1980
Running time: 39.46
Highest chart places: US: 35, UK: 48
Tracklisting: 1. 'Is That You?' (McMahon) 3.59, 2. 'Shandi' (Stanley, Poncia) 3.36, 3. 'Talk to Me' (Frehley) 4.00, 4. 'Naked City' (Simmons, Poncia, Kulick, Castro) 3.49, 5. 'What Makes the World Go 'Round' (Stanley, Poncia) 4.14, 6. 'Tomorrow' (Stanley, Poncia) 3.18, 7. 'Two Sides of the Coin' (Frehley) 3.16, 8. 'She's So European' (Simmons, Poncia) 3.24, 9. 'Easy As It Seems' (Stanley, Poncia) 3.24, 10. 'Torpedo Girl' (Frehley, Poncia) 3.44, 11. 'You're All That I Want' (Simmons, Poncia) 3.04

The 1970s are over, and so too the remit of this book, but Peter Criss's departure is fast approaching, and it is with the dissolution of the original four that we will take our leave. Better to find a natural break in our face-painted foursome's story rather than just abandoning them when the minute hand ticks into 1980.

As it transpires, Criss wasn't the first member of our cast to exit stage left, that honour falling to Casablanca founder Neil Bogart, a loveable rogue, a gambler, and a chancer whose time had come. It was Bogart that shipped the Kiss solos as platinum even though the demand was not there. In 1979, he pulled a similar stunt with *Take Me Home*, Cher's first album for the label. The singer was appearing on a late-night chat show when Bogart appeared to present her with a platinum record. The only problem was that said album had 'only' sold 700,000 copies, and not the required million to earn platinum status. Bogart's solution? Ship another 300,000 copies the next day. Like the surplus solos, they were returned unsold.

In 1977, fifty per cent of Casablanca had been bought over by PolyGram, the Dutch-German conglomerate that was well on its way to being a monolithic presence in the entertainment industry. In theory, that meant someone from PolyGram would be auditing Casablanca's figures, but whoever that was wasn't very good at their job. In his highly readable history of the record label, *And Party Every Day*, Larry Harris recalls Bogart telling him to add millions of bogus record sales to the quarterly sales projections that were being sent upstairs to PolyGram. Both Bogart and Harris knew these new figures were unattainable, but PolyGram didn't. As Harris so memorably phrased it, 'I think PolyGram's ignorance stemmed from the fact that we had painted the building so well they never realised they'd bought twelve coats of paint without a building underneath.'

Whether Bogart quit or was fired is yet another 'depends on who is telling the story' case, but Casablanca's excesses were legendary and Bogart's tampering with figures could not, and perhaps did not, remain hidden forever. Or perhaps Bogart just knew that the jig was up. Casablanca was primarily a disco label, and disco was dying. Parliament/Funkadelic and the Village People had seen their best days, and Donna Summer was so desperate to shake off her 'Queen of Disco' tag that she was prepared to leave Casablanca to do so. Either way, PolyGram bought out Bogart's fifty per cent, and he left the label he founded on 8 February 1980.

As it turns out, this had a huge positive impact on Kiss. Kiss had a 'key man' clause in their contract, meaning they could terminate their contract with Casablanca if their key man, in this case, Neil Bogart, left. Kiss handed in their notice less than a week after Bogart's departure. This was devastating news for PolyGram. Donna Summer had made good her threat and was now signed to the newly established Geffen Records. And now Kiss, who had just enjoyed worldwide success with *Dynasty* and 'I Was Made For Loving You', their biggest album and single in many territories, was following her out the door. PolyGram had bought a company that had just lost its two biggest assets.

Inevitably, they made Kiss an offer they couldn't refuse, and then the band's negotiators – Bill Aucoin, attorneys Paul Marshall and Stuart Silfen, and, especially, Howard Marks – made it even sweeter. The band signed a six-studio album deal with PolyGram subsidiary Phonogram International, and would receive $15 million up front, a $2m advance for each album, a flat rate of $1.20 per $8.98 album sold with a proportionate rate for cassette sales, and an advertising and promotions budget per album of $300,000 to $500,000 per album. 'You've just made these four boys rich', Marshall told Marks just before the contracts were signed, and indeed he had. No other band or act of the time had a deal comparable to it.

In the meantime, Kiss were in the studio working on their eighth album, *Unmasked*. Vini Poncia was once more behind the console and Anton Fig behind the drum kit, Poncia having again decided that Criss was not fit enough to play. According to Simmons, Poncia did ask Criss to come in to supply harmonies on some of the songs, but 'That didn't go very well either', suggesting Criss's vocal contributions weren't used. No other band member mentions this in their respective books, so it is possible Simmons is thinking of the *Dynasty* sessions. Despite appearing on the cover, Criss had no involvement with *Unmasked*, although he was still officially a member of the band.

As with *Dynasty*, the remaining band members were not operating as a cohesive unit. Simmons only appeared on five of the album's eleven tracks, with Frehley playing bass on his three songwriting contributions, and Stanley doing likewise on his songs 'Tomorrow' and 'Easy As It Seems.' Stanley's guitar tech Tom Harper plays bass on 'Shandi,' meaning that of the frontman's four efforts, Simmons only played on 'What Makes the World Go Round'. Stanley, meanwhile, plays lead guitar on most of his contributions, and supplies the solo to the non-band song 'Is That You?'

Dennis Woloch commissioned artist Victor Stabin to produce another striking cover, this time in the form of a comic strip in which a persistent reporter tries to photograph the members of Kiss without their trademark makeup. Each of the three lines of the strip was a separate painting, and when finished, the three were put together and photographed. The largest panel of the strip, when Kiss take off their masks to reveal the same faces underneath, was blown up to poster size and included in original copies of the album. There is one subtle difference between the original panel and the poster: in the former, Criss has his eyes open, but in the latter, he is winking. This was a visual joke added by Stabin at Woloch's suggestion, with the cartoon Criss knowingly acknowledging he hadn't played on the album.

Unmasked was released on 20 May, and, unusually, opened with a track not written within the band. 'Is That You?' was written by English singer-songwriter Gerard McMahon, a then up-and-comer who had fronted the band Gerard, possessors of one of the most laughingly underwhelming names in rock history. McMahon would later make his name writing songs for eighties films such as *Fast Times at Ridgemont High*, *All the Right Moves*, *Grandview, USA*, and *The Lost Boys*. With lyrics such as 'I hear you're cheatin' with my teacher', its two-verses-or-less structure, and Stanley's vocal, 'Is That You?' feels right at home on a Kiss album. Stanley subs for an *in absentia* Frehley on the solo.

According to Stanley in *Behind the Mask*, 'Shandi' was inspired by the Hollies' take on the Bruce Springsteen song '4th of July, Asbury Park (Sandy)', but the result is a mere shade of that song, one that has undergone surgery to remove all traces of both 'life' and 'soul'. What we have instead is a slab of yacht rock so bloated it could be the poster boy for the genre. Dave Marshall of Radio Clyde possibly made it his record of the week. 'That song didn't necessarily sound like Kiss…,' bemoaned the starry-eyed one to Ken Sharp. No foolin', considering the musicians on the track are Holly Knight, Vini Poncia, Anton Fig, and Tom Harper, or in other words, not Kiss. Frehley *is* there, but not in his customary axe-wielding role; instead, he is relegated to the background, where he vainly tries adding acoustic warmth to this slick, sickly monstrosity.

A natural question arises when listening to 'Shandi': 'Who buys this drivel?' Millions of people, it transpires, most of them Argentinean, where astonishingly it claimed pole position, and Norwegian (#4), Australian (#5), and New Zealand (#6). It was less loved at home, stalling at forty-seven.

As with the previous album, Frehley supplies three tracks, the first of which is 'Talk to Me'. Anyone wondering what the Stones would have sounded like if they had come together as a post-punk power pop band need wonder no more; they would have sounded *this* good. 'Talk to Me' was the second single released from *Unmasked*, and the first Kiss A-side penned by Frehley. It cracked the top ten in Switzerland and the top forty in Australia, Germany, and the Netherlands.

Simmons' first contribution, 'Naked City' takes its title and paraphrases a line ('There are ten million stories…') from the late '50s, early '60s television show. As with his *Dynasty* numbers, 'Naked City' is a marked improvement on his pre-solo album material, and like all the songs thus far, it is dressed in a shiny pop sheen rather than a hard rock edge. Simmons even tries out his falsetto, and it works just fine. The song was written by Simmons, Poncia, and a couple of recurring guests in the Kiss story, Peppy Castro and Bob Kulick. Kulick played additional guitars on the song, but the solo was performed by Frehley.

'What Makes the World Go Round' is Stanley's second song on the album and demonstrates an increased sophistication to the Starchild's songwriting. However, 'sophisticated' doesn't necessarily equate with 'exciting,' and while far superior to the execrable 'Shandi', this is a song pulled from a few drawers down. The same cannot be said of 'Tomorrow', a power pop classic with exquisite harmonies, a bright lead guitar line in the chorus courtesy of Frehley, and some judiciously placed hand claps. Crisp and catchy, this, along with Frehley's thematically similar 'Talk To Me', is the highlight of the album and one of Stanley's best. Kiss obviously disagree, as, astonishingly, it has never been played live.

'Two Sides of the Coin' is a mid-tempo Frehley rocker with sweet lyrics celebrating the joy of finding the right life partner. At least, that is how I read it. How disappointing then, to find that, according to the song's author, it *is* about finding the right person, and then cheating on them, the two sides of the coin being your wife and your girlfriend. This track is the lesser of Frehley's three songs but is a perfectly acceptable tune if you can get by the misogyny at its core.

'She's So European' is another decent effort from Simmons and Poncia, although it is slightly marred by a weedy keyboard part that is so eighties it could have been played by Max Headroom (Holly Knight is, in fact, the guilty party). The keyboards are equally as prominent and as weedy on 'Easy as It Seems', Stanley's final contribution to the album, co-written by Poncia. For the record, Poncia gets a writing credit on all songs except McMahon's 'Is That You?' and the two Frehley songs. Poncia does get a co-writing credit on Frehley's final song, the silly-in-a-good-way 'Torpedo Girl'. It sounds like the Space Ace has docked with the Parliament/Funkadelic mothership, thanks to Fig and Frehley's funky playing on drums and bass, respectively, and shows that Frehley wasn't afraid to have a little fun in the studio. Fig shines throughout the album, but he really seems to click when working with Ace. *Unmasked* concludes with 'You're All That I Want', a surprisingly sweet Simmons song with nary a horny old demon in sight.

The album peaked at 35 in the United States, their worst performing record since 1974's *Hotter Than Hell*. On the other hand, it was a massive success elsewhere, topping the New Zealand and Norwegian album charts and going top five in Australia, Germany, and Austria, and top twenty in Canada, Japan, Sweden, and Holland.

Despite this success, Stanley was brutal when rating the album in *Behind the Mask*, calling *Unmasked* 'a pretty crappy album', although he singled out 'Tomorrow' as being 'a really great song'. Simmons was equally harsh when talking to Mike Gittar of *Kerrang!* in 1993: 'It's a shitty album. I'd be ashamed of playing it for my mother or anybody else'. It remains one of the most divisive entries in the Kiss catalogue – a trawl through the numerous 'Kiss albums ranked' webpages reveal it usually lurks in the lower reaches – and most fans decry it as being too polished and poppy, and 'not Kiss enough'. Thank the gods David Bowie fans were more open-minded, or we might never have got *Station to Station* or *Low*.

Unmasked is a power-pop classic, and while Kiss fans – and Kiss themselves – never saw the band in that genre, they were always more aligned to the Beatles, the Who and the Raspberries than Led Zeppelin or Deep Purple. Considering these influences, not to mention the decline in sales for many a Seventies hard rocker, the impact of the new wave, and their maturing songwriting abilities and musicianship, perhaps *Unmasked* was the only album they could have conceived in 1980.

Two days before *Unmasked* was released, Peter Criss was fired from Kiss (or quit; as so often with Kiss, it depends on who you are listening to), but because he still had some contractual obligations to fulfil his departure wasn't announced to the press. The most pressing of those obligations was a promotional video for 'Shandi', which was being released as the album's first single. The video was directed by John Goodhue, who had been responsible for the 'I Was Made for Lovin' You' and 'Sure No Something' clips, and was shot at the since-demolished Dick Clark Westchester Theatre in Tarrytown, New York, in mid-June.

The video follows roughly the same plot as the album cover, but rather than a reporter it is an unidentified young woman, only ever seen in the shadows, that sneaks backstage to see what the band look like without their makeup. After they perform the song onstage (what *is* Paul wearing?), they return to their dressing room, change into their civvies (no, what *is* Paul *wearing*?) and depart. When they reach the stage door, the woman shouts 'Kiss', and they turn around to reveal that they are still wearing their makeup, suggesting, as with the penultimate panel on the album cover, that that is their real faces.

This promotional film was Criss's last appearance with the other three original band members until the *MTV Unplugged* gig fifteen years later. 'At the end of the day', wrote Stanley in *Face the Music*, 'he took his makeup case with him and left. It wasn't tearful, but it was a big moment. Oddly enough, he didn't seem to care. He was likely in his own drug haze and saw this as his big opportunity. In his mind, he wrote the biggest song we ever had, and now he was free to go out and become the big star he should be'.

Criss remembers it differently. 'When we finished (the video shoot), they rushed to the dressing room and took their makeup off in record time. Ace and Paul walked out without even saying goodbye to me'. Criss asked Simmons if he could have his bass as a keepsake of his time with the band, and Simmons agreed. 'After he left, I sat alone in front of my mirror. I just felt so bad that they had left me sitting there alone, like a piece of dirt. My three brothers in arms. I cried so hard that all my makeup washed off my face. For the last time'.

The press was finally informed of Criss's departure, many of whom inevitably deemed it the 'end of an era', and so it appeared to the band's legion of fans, so successful was Kiss in casting their illusion of unity. It was not until much later that the truth would emerge, that Criss was not on the last two Kiss albums save for one track he wrote, and that the era really ended three years earlier with the release of *Love Gun*, the last project the four members of the band worked on together.

The immediate effect of Criss's departure was the cancellation of a huge European tour, as well a handful of dates in Mexico. Some of the European dates were rescheduled for autumn (but not the show at the Royal Highland Showground in Edinburgh, for which I had tickets, so thanks for nothing, guys). Also pencilled in for November and December was the band's first tour of Australia and New Zealand, where they would be greeted with scenes resembling Beatlemania. Despite the poor showing of *Unmasked* in the American charts, no one in the Kiss organisation could have foreseen their upcoming spectacular fall from grace in their homeland. By returning to Europe and playing Australasia, Kiss were making connections with new audiences that would see them through a lean 1980s.

But that is the story for another book.

Epilogue: What Happened Next.

Kiss's priority was to find a replacement for Criss, which they did in Paul Caravello, a stove repairman that asked the band for their autographs at his audition in case he didn't see them again. Because of Kiss's one-Paul-per-band rule, Caravello rechristened himself Eric Carr. After rejecting a hideous Hawk makeup and costume design, Carr adopted the role of the Fox. The Fox made his debut on 25 July 1980 at the Palladium in New York City and played on seven full-length albums as well as new songs on compilations *Killers* and *Smashes, Thrashes, and Hits*. He was diagnosed with cancer in early February 1991 and could only contribute backing vocals to one track on that year's *Revenge* album. Eric Carr succumbed to his illness on 24 November 1991, the same day as Queen's Freddie Mercury died, and was replaced by Eric Singer, who had subbed for him on *Revenge*.

Carr's first album with Kiss, *Music from 'The Elder'*, proved to be Frehley's swansong with the band. Whereas Criss had been a partner in Kiss, Carr was merely an employee and had no say in band decisions. As such, Frehley often found himself at odds with Simmons and Stanley, and this shift in the balance of power became an increasing source of discontent for the guitarist. For example, Frehley consistently voted against *Music from 'The Elder'*, a soft rock concept album with orchestral elements and a half-baked 'story' that made James Cameron's *Avatar* seem intricate, but Stanley and Simmons insisted on moving forward, convinced this project would establish their reputations as serious artists. It didn't; *Theme from 'The Elder'* was a critical and commercial flop, peaking at 75 on the *Billboard* chart, and would rival *Phantom of the Park* as a source of embarrassment for the band. It didn't help that Bob Ezrin, who Frehley did not get along with, was hired to produce the album. The Space Ace tendered his resignation in 1982 and was succeeded first by Vinnie Vincent and then Mark St. John before the band settled on Bruce Kulick, brother of long-time ally Bob Kulick.

Aside from losing their mercurial guitarist, Frehley's departure meant that PolyGram could renegotiate their terms with the band as their contract stipulated that Kiss included the three remaining original members following Criss's exit. With Ace gone, that original contract was null and void, and that sweet deal including $15 million upfront, $2m advance for each album, and 13% of album sales went with him. Furthermore, the performance of *Music from 'The Elder'* was factored into the renegotiations, and Kiss had to settle for a deal more befitting a band showing signs of decline.

The following year, 1983, Kiss took an extreme step to address that decline by taking off their trademark makeup and costumes, and the gamble worked. They were newsworthy again and released a string of gold and platinum-selling albums in the 1980s. Although they played to their biggest ever audience, 130,000, at the Maracanã Stadium in Rio de Janeiro in 1983, they also toured more extensively in Europe, playing venues like the Glasgow Apollo (capacity 3,500) and Newcastle City Hall (2,135), venues that would never have been considered in their '70s heyday. This strategy also paid off, earning them top ten placings in the UK for *Lick It Up* and *Crazy Nights*, another circumstance inconceivable the previous decade.

Peter Criss launched a solo career immediately after leaving Kiss, but the two albums he released in the 1980s, *Out of Control* (1980) and *Let Me Rock You* (1982) failed to make an impact. Ace Frehley had greater success with the release of *Frehley's Comet*, also the name of his new band, in 1987. This album made *Billboard* 43, although its successor, *Second Sighting*, only reached 81, and his second album under his own name, *Trouble Walkin'* (1989), failed to breach the top one hundred.

Neil Bogart started a new label, Boardwalk, in 1980. Its first release was *Sequel*, Harry Chapin's final album before his death in a car accident in 1981. Boardwalk's biggest-selling record was *I Love Rock 'n' Roll* by Joan Jett and the Blackhearts, which reached number two on the *Billboard* chart and was a success internationally. Bogart died of cancer and lymphoma on 8 May 1982, aged 39.

Bill Aucoin and Kiss parted company in 1982, after which he managed Billy Idol to international success, followed by an eclectic range of unsuccessful acts into the new century. His last 'name' act was Finnish hard rockers and Gene Simmons wannabees Lordi, whom Aucoin managed until his death from prostate cancer in 2010.

Sean Delaney, often credited as 'the fifth member of Kiss,' worked with various Aucoin acts such as Starz, Piper, and Toby Beau, before forming the Skatt Brothers in 1979. They released two unsuccessful albums. Improbably, Delaney moved to Sunderland, England, in the early 2000s to manage English country duo, Smith & Jackson. He died of complications due to diabetes in 2003 and is buried in Orem, Utah. The first names of the four original members of Kiss are engraved on the bottom right of his tombstone. None of them attended his funeral, although Aucoin and Lydia Criss did.

As he had done with the Catman's solo album, Stan Penridge co-wrote most of the material on Criss's post-Kiss *Out of Control* platter and in 1983, formed the short-lived Criss-Penridge Alliance with the former Kiss drummer. The band split up the following year, and Penridge moved to Austin, Texas, where he became an independent music producer for local acts. He died unexpectedly in 2001.

Frequent Kiss collaborator Bob Kulick formed the moderately successful band Balance in 1981 with another familiar face in the Kiss story, former Blue Magoo Peppy Castro. He also played on studio albums by Diana Ross and Michael Bolton, was a long-serving member of Meat Loaf's touring band, and played on Paul Stanley's 1989 solo club tour. He passed away in 2020 from heart disease.

Peter Criss decided to attend a Kiss Konvention in 1995 so that his daughter Jenilee could gain a better appreciation of what he had achieved in the past. When Simmons got wind of this he got in touch with Criss, saying there was no way a founding member of Kiss was going to wander around the convention like a regular punter; he should be with the band, perhaps even sing a few songs. According to Criss's autobiography, the day was a triumph, his daughter 'blown away' by the adulation accorded to him.

This led to Criss and Frehley both being invited to perform when Kiss got the *MTV Unplugged* gig. The current line-up of Stanley, Simmons, Bruce Kulick and Eric Singer performed the main set, and then Criss and Frehley were invited onstage to rapturous applause. The four original members did two songs, '2000 Man' and 'Beth', the first time they had performed together since 1979 and the first time they had performed without the face paint. Kulick and Singer then re-joined them for a rousing finale of 'Nothin' to Lose' and 'Rock and Roll All Nite.' The overwhelmingly positive reaction pointed to one obvious conclusion; it was time to put the original band back together again.

At the 38th Grammy Awards on 28 February 1996, Tupac Shakur invited the four original members on stage to present the Best Pop Performance by a Duo or Group with Vocal Award, and they showed up in makeup and *Love Gun*-era costumes. The Reunion Tour was officially announced on 16 April.

The tour was a massive success, catapulting Kiss back to the top, and was quickly followed by the *Psycho Circus* Tour and the Farewell Tour. As the tours progressed, however, the old ego trips, insecurities, and incidents of substance abuse re-emerged. Criss left the band on 31

January 2001, unhappy with his salary and too focused on how much everyone else was getting paid. That he was now earning millions – millions he didn't earn in his years out of the band – didn't seem to occur to him. He was replaced by Eric Singer, who, in a move that proved controversial with fans, wore the Catman makeup. Frehley left at the end of the Farewell tour, his last gig being the closing ceremony of the 2002 Winter Olympics at Salt Lake City, Utah.

Despite its name, the Farewell Tour wasn't the end; the show, it seems, must go on. Tommy Thayer, once of Kiss tribute band Cold Gin and later in '80s rockers Black 'n' Blue, had worked for Kiss in various capacities, not least in getting Criss and Frehley up to speed for the Reunion Tour. When Kiss were offered the opportunity to do a co-headline tour with old rivals Aerosmith in 2003, they approached Frehley about re-joining, but when the Space Ace knocked them back, they turned to Thayer to become the new Spaceman, 'Space Tommy' not quite having the same ring. For reasons known only unto them, the Aerosmith camp insisted that Kiss have at least three of their original members, so the original Cat came back. This line-up played some dates in Australia, including one with the Melbourne Symphony Orchestra, which was recorded for the *Kiss Symphony: Alive IV* album, before embarking on the US *Rocksimus Maximus* Tour with Aerosmith. Criss left Kiss for the third and final time in 2004 when his contract was not renewed. He retired in 2017.

Frehley re-established his solo career and released a string of charting albums, one of which, 2014's *Space Invader*, even cracked the *Billboard* top ten. He has had the most successful career as a solo artist than any other member of Kiss.

Current Kiss members Eric Singer and Tommy Thayer are now the band's longest-serving drummer and lead guitarist respectively, and both played on the 21st-century albums *Sonic Boom* (2009) and *Monster* (2012). The current line-up of Stanley, Simmons, Singer, and Thayer are on their *End of the Road* Tour, which started on 31 January 2019 and will finish on 30 November 2022 in Tokyo, after which, after fifty years of triumphs and tribulations, the curtain will fall for the final time on the world's most recognisable rock brand. Despite the misleading Farewell Tour of two decades earlier, both Stanley and Simmons are adamant that this time it truly is The End.

Bibliography

Ballard, R. (2020) *It's Good to be Here: Scenes from a Life in Music*. BMG Rights Management.
Bangs, L. (1977) 'Kiss: Rock and Roll Over'. Circus magazine.
Brod, D. (2020). *They Just Seem a Little Weird: How Kiss, Cheap Trick, Aerosmith, and Starz Remade Rock and Roll*, Hachette Books, New York
Campion, J. (2015). *Shout It Out Loud: The Story of Kiss's* Destroyer *and the Making of an American Icon*. Backbeat Books, Milwaukee
Criss, P & Sloman, L. (2012). *Makeup to Breakup: My Life In and Out of Kiss*. Scribner, New York
Dimery, R., et al. (2006). *1001 Albums You Must Hear Before You Die*. Quintet Publishing Limited, London
Doherty, H. (1976) "Kiss: *Destroyer* (Casablanca)". *Melody Maker*.
Frehley, A. (2011). *No Regrets: A Rock and Roll Memior*. Simon & Schuster UK Ltd, London
Gill, J. (2015), *Gene, Ace, Peter & Paul: A Detailed Exploration of the 1978 Kiss Solo Albums*, KissFAQ.com Books
Harris, L. *et al* (2009). *And Party Every Day: The Inside Story of Casablanca Records*. Backbeat Books, Milwaukee
Hiatt, B. (2014). 'Kiss Forever: 40 Years of Feuds and Fury'. Rolling Stone.
Howe, S. (2012). *Marvel Comics: The Untold Story*. HarperCollins, New York
Khoury, G. (2016). *Comic Book Fever: A Celebration of Comics 1976-1986*. TwoMorrows Publishing, Raliegh, North Carolina
Leaf, D. & Sharp, K. (2004). *Kiss: Behind the Mask; The Official Authorised Biography*, Auren Press Ltd., London
Lendt, C. K. (1997). *Kiss and Sell: The Making of a Supergroup. Billboard* Books, New York
Sharp, K. (2021). *The Story of Kiss Destroyer*. Liner notes for the *Destroyer* 45th Anniversary Deluxe Boxset. Universal Music.
Sharp, K. with Stanley. P & Simmons, G. (2014). *Nothin' to Lose: The Making of Kiss 1972-1975*. It Books / Harper Collins, New York
Simmons, G. (2003) *Kiss and Make-Up*. Arrow / Random House, New York
Stanley, P. (2014). *Face the Music: A Life Exposed*. Harper One / Harper Collins, New York

Websites

Much of the information regarding the Kiss album cover designs comes from Claudio Bergamin's excellent series of YouTube interviews with Casablanca Record's art director Dennis Woloch.

rocksbackpages.com
apoplife.com
kissconcerthistory.com
kissfaq.com
legendaryrockinterviews.com
loudersound.com
lynchristopher.com
mentalfloss.com
metalexpressradio.com
nytimes.com
printmag.com
thebeautifultimes.com
usatoday.com

Warren Zevon - *on track*
every album, every song

Peter Gallagher
Paperback
128 pages
40 colour photographs
978-1-78951-170-2
£15.99
$22.95

Every album and every song by this underappreciated American songwriter.

Bruce Springsteen called him 'one of the great, great American songwriters', Jackson Browne hailed him as 'the first and foremost proponent of song noir' and Stephen King once said that if he could write like Zevon, he 'would be a happy guy'. The list of artists that lined up to appear on his records include Springsteen, Neil Young, Bob Dylan, Dave Gilmour and Emmylou Harris. So how is it that most people, if they have heard of Warren Zevon at all, know him only as 'that werewolves guy'?

This book goes beyond that solitary hit single to examine all aspects of Zevon's multifaceted, five-decade career, from his beginnings in the slightly psychedelic folk duo Lyme and Cybelle, through to his commercial breakthrough in the late Seventies with *Excitable Boy*, his critically acclaimed late Eighties comeback *Sentimental Hygiene*, his decline into cult obscurity, and his triumphant if heart-breaking final testament *The Wind* released just prior to his death in 2003.

Along the way, the reader will discover one of rock's consummate balladeers, as well as his cast of characters, which include doomed drug dealers, psychopathic adolescents, outlaws of the Old West, BDSM fetishists, ghostly gunslingers and, yes, lycanthropes unleashed on the streets of London.

Also available from Sonicbond

On Track series

Alan Parsons Project – Steve Swift 978-1-78952-154-2
Tori Amos – Lisa Torem 978-1-78952-142-9
Asia – Peter Braidis 978-1-78952-099-6
Badfinger – Robert Day-Webb 978-1-878952-176-4
Barclay James Harvest – Keith and Monica Domone 978-1-78952-067-5
The Beatles – Andrew Wild 978-1-78952-009-5
The Beatles Solo 1969-1980 – Andrew Wild 978-1-78952-030-9
Blue Oyster Cult – Jacob Holm-Lupo 978-1-78952-007-1
Blur – Matt Bishop – 978-178952-164-1
Marc Bolan and T.Rex – Peter Gallagher 978-1-78952-124-5
Kate Bush – Bill Thomas 978-1-78952-097-2
Camel – Hamish Kuzminski 978-1-78952-040-8
Caravan – Andy Boot 978-1-78952-127-6
Cardiacs – Eric Benac 978-1-78952-131-3
Eric Clapton Solo – Andrew Wild 978-1-78952-141-2
The Clash – Nick Assirati 978-1-78952-077-4
Crosby, Stills and Nash – Andrew Wild 978-1-78952-039-2
The Damned – Morgan Brown 978-1-78952-136-8
Deep Purple and Rainbow 1968-79 – Steve Pilkington 978-1-78952-002-6
Dire Straits – Andrew Wild 978-1-78952-044-6
The Doors – Tony Thompson 978-1-78952-137-5
Dream Theater – Jordan Blum 978-1-78952-050-7
Electric Light Orchestra – Barry Delve 978-1-78952-152-8
Elvis Costello and The Attractions – Georg Purvis 978-1-78952-129-0
Emerson Lake and Palmer – Mike Goode 978-1-78952-000-2
Fairport Convention – Kevan Furbank 978-1-78952-051-4
Peter Gabriel – Graeme Scarfe 978-1-78952-138-2
Genesis – Stuart MacFarlane 978-1-78952-005-7
Gentle Giant – Gary Steel 978-1-78952-058-3
Gong – Kevan Furbank 978-1-78952-082-8
Hall and Oates – Ian Abrahams 978-1-78952-167-2
Hawkwind – Duncan Harris 978-1-78952-052-1
Peter Hammill – Richard Rees Jones 978-1-78952-163-4
Roy Harper – Opher Goodwin 978-1-78952-130-6
Jimi Hendrix – Emma Stott 978-1-78952-175-7
The Hollies – Andrew Darlington 978-1-78952-159-7
Iron Maiden – Steve Pilkington 978-1-78952-061-3
Jefferson Airplane – Richard Butterworth 978-1-78952-143-6
Jethro Tull – Jordan Blum 978-1-78952-016-3
Elton John in the 1970s – Peter Kearns 978-1-78952-034-7
The Incredible String Band – Tim Moon 978-1-78952-107-8
Iron Maiden – Steve Pilkington 978-1-78952-061-3
Judas Priest – John Tucker 978-1-78952-018-7
Kansas – Kevin Cummings 978-1-78952-057-6
The Kinks – Martin Hutchinson 978-1-78952-172-6

Korn – Matt Karpe 978-1-78952-153-5
Led Zeppelin – Steve Pilkington 978-1-78952-151-1
Level 42 – Matt Philips 978-1-78952-102-3
Little Feat – 978-1-78952-168-9
Aimee Mann – Jez Rowden 978-1-78952-036-1
Joni Mitchell – Peter Kearns 978-1-78952-081-1
The Moody Blues – Geoffrey Feakes 978-1-78952-042-2
Motorhead – Duncan Harris 978-1-78952-173-3
Mike Oldfield – Ryan Yard 978-1-78952-060-6
Opeth – Jordan Blum 978-1-78-952-166-5
Tom Petty – Richard James 978-1-78952-128-3
Porcupine Tree – Nick Holmes 978-1-78952-144-3
Queen – Andrew Wild 978-1-78952-003-3
Radiohead – William Allen 978-1-78952-149-8
Renaissance – David Detmer 978-1-78952-062-0
The Rolling Stones 1963-80 – Steve Pilkington 978-1-78952-017-0
The Smiths and Morrissey – Tommy Gunnarsson 978-1-78952-140-5
Status Quo the Frantic Four Years – Richard James 978-1-78952-160-3
Steely Dan – Jez Rowden 978-1-78952-043-9
Steve Hackett – Geoffrey Feakes 978-1-78952-098-9
Thin Lizzy – Graeme Stroud 978-1-78952-064-4
Toto – Jacob Holm-Lupo 978-1-78952-019-4
U2 – Eoghan Lyng 978-1-78952-078-1
UFO – Richard James 978-1-78952-073-6
The Who – Geoffrey Feakes 978-1-78952-076-7
Roy Wood and the Move – James R Turner 978-1-78952-008-8
Van Der Graaf Generator – Dan Coffey 978-1-78952-031-6
Yes – Stephen Lambe 978-1-78952-001-9
Frank Zappa 1966 to 1979 – Eric Benac 978-1-78952-033-0
Warren Zevon – Peter Gallagher 978-1-78952-170-2
10CC – Peter Kearns 978-1-78952-054-5

Decades Series

The Bee Gees in the 1960s – Andrew Mon Hughes et al 978-1-78952-148-1
The Bee Gees in the 1970s – Andrew Mon Hughes et al 978-1-78952-179-5
Black Sabbath in the 1970s – Chris Sutton 978-1-78952-171-9
Britpop – Peter Richard Adams and Matt Pooler 978-1-78952-169-6
Alice Cooper in the 1970s – Chris Sutton 978-1-78952-104-7
Curved Air in the 1970s – Laura Shenton 978-1-78952-069-9
Bob Dylan in the 1980s – Don Klees 978-1-78952-157-3
Fleetwood Mac in the 1970s – Andrew Wild 978-1-78952-105-4
Focus in the 1970s – Stephen Lambe 978-1-78952-079-8
Free and Bad Company in the 1970s – John Van der Kiste 978-1-78952-178-8
Genesis in the 1970s – Bill Thomas 978178952-146-7
George Harrison in the 1970s – Eoghan Lyng 978-1-78952-174-0
Marillion in the 1980s – Nathaniel Webb 978-1-78952-065-1
Mott the Hoople and Ian Hunter in the 1970s – John Van der Kiste 978-1-78-952-162-7

Pink Floyd In The 1970s – Georg Purvis 978-1-78952-072-9
Tangerine Dream in the 1970s – Stephen Palmer 978-1-78952-161-0
The Sweet in the 1970s – Darren Johnson 978-1-78952-139-9
Uriah Heep in the 1970s – Steve Pilkington 978-1-78952-103-0
Yes in the 1980s – Stephen Lambe with David Watkinson 978-1-78952-125-2

On Screen series

Carry On… – Stephen Lambe 978-1-78952-004-0
David Cronenberg – Patrick Chapman 978-1-78952-071-2
Doctor Who: The David Tennant Years – Jamie Hailstone 978-1-78952-066-8
James Bond – Andrew Wild – 978-1-78952-010-1
Monty Python – Steve Pilkington 978-1-78952-047-7
Seinfeld Seasons 1 to 5 – Stephen Lambe 978-1-78952-012-5

Other Books

1967: A Year In Psychedelic Rock – Kevan Furbank 978-1-78952-155-9
1970: A Year In Rock – John Van der Kiste 978-1-78952-147-4
1973: The Golden Year of Progressive Rock 978-1-78952-165-8
Babysitting A Band On The Rocks – G.D. Praetorius 978-1-78952-106-1
Eric Clapton Sessions – Andrew Wild 978-1-78952-177-1
Derek Taylor: For Your Radioactive Children – Andrew Darlington 978-1-78952-038-5
The Golden Road: The Recording History of The Grateful Dead – John Kilbride 978-1-78952-156-6
Iggy and The Stooges On Stage 1967-1974 – Per Nilsen 978-1-78952-101-6
Jon Anderson and the Warriors – the road to Yes – David Watkinson 978-1-78952-059-0
Nu Metal: A Definitive Guide – Matt Karpe 978-1-78952-063-7
Tommy Bolin: In and Out of Deep Purple – Laura Shenton 978-1-78952-070-5
Maximum Darkness – Deke Leonard 978-1-78952-048-4
Maybe I Should've Stayed In Bed – Deke Leonard 978-1-78952-053-8
The Twang Dynasty – Deke Leonard 978-1-78952-049-1

and many more to come!

Would you like to write for Sonicbond Publishing?

At Sonicbond Publishing we are always on the look-out for authors, particularly for our two main series:

On Track. Mixing fact with in depth analysis, the On Track series examines the work of a particular musical artist or group. All genres are considered from easy listening and jazz to 60s soul to 90s pop, via rock and metal.

On Screen. This series looks at the world of film and television. Subjects considered include directors, actors and writers, as well as entire television and film series. As with the On Track series, we balance fact with analysis.

While professional writing experience would, of course, be an advantage the most important qualification is to have real enthusiasm and knowledge of your subject. First-time authors are welcomed, but the ability to write well in English is essential.

Sonicbond Publishing has distribution throughout Europe and North America, and all books are also published in E-book form. Authors will be paid a royalty based on sales of their book.

Further details are available from www.sonicbondpublishing.co.uk. To contact us, complete the contact form there or email info@sonicbondpublishing.co.uk